CONTEMPORARY
CATHOLIC
SEXUALITY

CONTEMPORARY CATHOLIC SEXUALITY

WHAT IS TAUGHT AND WHAT IS PRACTICED

John E. Perito

A Crossroad Book
The Crossroad Publishing Company
New York

The Crossroad Publishing Company
481 Eighth Avenue, New York, NY 10001

Printed in the United States of America

Library of Congress Cataloging-in-Publication Data
Perito, John E.
    CONTEMPORARY CATHOLIC SEXUALITY : what is taught and
what is practiced / by John E. Perito.
        p.   cm.
    Includes bibliographical references.
    ISBN 0-8245-1968-X (alk. paper)
    1. Sex – Religious aspects – Catholic Church.   2. Psychiatry and religion.
I. Title.
BX1795.S48P47 2002
241'.66 – dc21

2001003909

To my wife, Pat,
for her faith, love, and unswerving support
over the past forty-five years

To the memory of my parents, Lucille and John,
who discovered true love early on
in their own short lives

To my aunt Lucille,
who parented me from the time
I was fourteen

To my children, Paul and Judi,
and grandchildren, Dylan, Zoe, Logan, and Chris,
who fill my life with love and delight

To my sister Mary Ann,
who has always found my better side

Contents

Foreword   9

Prologue   17

Acknowledgments   23

Part I
BASICS

1. Introduction   29
2. Theology, Psychology, and Sexuality   33
3. Psychodynamics and Sexuality   41

Part II
ISSUES OF MORALITY

4. Sexuality and Conscience Formation   69
5. Sexuality and Masturbation   88
6. Sexuality and Homosexuality   94
7. Sexuality, Contraception, and Reproduction 102

Part III
PRACTICAL QUESTIONS

8. Sexuality and Spirituality   115
9. Sexuality, Fantasy, and Tradition   134
10. Sexuality and Celibacy   140
11. Sexuality and Marriage   148
12. Sexuality and the Roman Catholic Priesthood 160
13. Sexuality and Aging   167
14. Sexuality and Pedophilia   171

Epilogue   187

Notes   191

Foreword

"After taking this course, I understand the logic behind the Catholic Church's positions. I may not agree with all of them but at least now I see a reason for these positions. But there is some questionable logic at work here...."

This quotation comes from the take-home examination of a non-Catholic student in a course, "Bioethics from a Christian Perspective," which I taught to undergraduates at Southern Methodist University. This reaction, however, is common to many Catholics and non-Catholics alike. Catholic teaching on bioethics and sexuality often comes across as a command from church authority without any logic or reason behind it, but this authoritative teaching also claims to be based on reason. In reality, an inherent tension exists in Catholic moral teaching in general and in sexual ethics in particular between the insistence that such teachings are based on natural law but are also proposed as authoritative teaching to be followed by all Catholics.

In the last few decades the Vatican's insistence on a more centralized and authoritative approach has exacerbated this inherent tension between what is taught authoritatively and what is based on natural law and human reason.

The resulting tension exists on many different levels throughout the church. Everyone recognizes that a vast majority of Catholics in practice do not accept the church's teaching condemning artificial contraception for spouses. Likewise, many Catholics disagree with the teaching on masturbation, homosexuality, and divorce. Pope John Paul II himself has recognized this reality as illustrated in the discussion at the Consistory of Cardinals held in May of 2001. This glaring discrepancy between authoritative hierarchical teaching and Catholic practice raises very serious questions on a pastoral level for the Catholic Church and its future.

On a theological level, many Catholic moral theologians have expressed public dissent with some of the existing church teachings and the natural law basis for these teachings. However, the Roman Curia, the Congregation for the Doctrine of the Faith, and the pope have reacted by strongly reaffirming all these teachings and occasionally taking action of various kinds to prohibit and prevent theological dissent on these issues.

The tension exists even more broadly on the educational level in Catholic schools and religious education. The textbooks, ever faithful to the hierarchical teaching, continue to teach and defend all the existing teachings. However, many teachers have their own personal disagreements with some of these teachings, but they are afraid to voice their positions in the classroom. Thus, the teachers often find themselves in a very difficult personal bind.

Without doubt, our age in many ways is anti-authoritarian. The danger in our society springs from a one-sided individualism that sees no role whatsoever for authority. However, every social reality — from the family, to the union, to the corporation, to the government — needs authority in order to direct its members to the common good. Church authority has the function of directing people with the assistance of the Holy Spirit in matters of faith and morality. But church authority in the form of the hierarchical authority in sexual issues has lost respect among many Catholics. The danger is that as a result hierarchical teaching authority will become rejected across the board. We Catholics who disagree with certain hierarchical teachings are not anti-authority; in fact, we are trying to strengthen and support the proper and necessary role of authority in the church.

Not only is authority itself suffering in the present situation, but also many teachers in the church fail to point out the good things that the church and its tradition have to say on issues such as sexuality. Frankly, I think the church has many good things to say here, and I certainly do not want to accept everything that is taking place in our society today. We can learn many things from our society, but we also have to criticize some aspects. A few years ago I asked a group of fifteen diocesan priests when was the last time they talked about sexuality in any forum. There was a general silence, and one by one they admitted that none of them had talked about it in the last ten years. These priests obviously had their personal disagreements with some of the church's teaching in these areas and felt the only way they could deal with the tension was to remain quiet about the whole area of sexuality.

What can be done about the present situation with all its tensions? Many diverse responses exist within the church today. Some maintain the present hierarchical church teaching is totally correct and nothing should be changed. I disagree. The present teaching on a number of issues (by no means all) should be changed — e.g., artificial contraception, masturbation, homosexuality, divorce, and remarriage. In my judgment such changes would be in keeping with the best of the Catholic theological tradition. How can I justify such an assertion?

As pointed out, an inherent tension exists between the claim that hierarchical teaching is authoritative and is also based on human reason. Where there is a conflict what prevails — authority or reason? Thousands of books and articles have dealt with this question. In this context one aspect of the Catholic moral tradition stands out — the insistence on an intrinsic morality. Thomas Aquinas asked the question: Is something commanded because it is good or is it good because it is commanded? One might dismiss this as an esoteric scholastic debate that has no practical relevance. But in reality this is a significant question with many important practical ramifications. According to Thomas Aquinas, something is commanded because it is good. Authority must conform itself to the true and the good. Authority does not make something right or wrong. In technical language, morality is intrinsic. Extrinsic authority or commands cannot make something right or wrong. The Catholic tradition, in accord with Thomas Aquinas, has recognized at least in theory that morality is intrinsic. The teaching authority must conform itself to the truth.

But another very significant question logically arises: What is moral truth and how do we determine it? The Catholic answer is natural law. Natural law in its most general formulation claims that human reason reflecting on what God has made can determine how God wants us to use it. The question for the believer is: How do we know what God wants us to do? Natural law illustrates the Catholic insistence on mediation. We do not go immediately to God and ask her what to do. According to the natural law, God's reason has formulated a plan for the world according to which God created all things. God gave us our reason, which can look at and examine what God has made and determine what is God's plan and how God wants us to act. The Roman Catholic tradition recognizes that human reason reflecting on human nature can arrive at true moral wisdom and knowledge.

But the important question arises, what do you mean by human reason and human nature? The understanding of human nature undergirding the hierarchical teaching in sexuality suffers from three defects — a faculty teleology, a two- or three-layered anthropology, and biologism or physicalism.

First, a faculty teleology. Teleology is an ethical method that understands the good as the end toward which we strive. Something is good if it brings me toward that end and bad if it prevents my arrival at it. The first question treated by Aquinas in his discussion of morality in the *Summa Theologiae* concerns the ultimate end of human beings. A faculty teleology looks at the end or purpose of the individual human faculty or power which determines how the faculty should be used. For example, the purpose of speech is to put on my lips what is in my mind. Lying is wrong because I put on my lips what is not in my mind. I use the faculty of speech against its God-given purpose. The end or purpose of sexuality or the sexual faculty is the procreation of offspring and the expression and development of the love union of the spouses (before Vatican II the latter was called the secondary purpose or end of marriage). Every sexual act, therefore, must be open to procreation and expressive of love. Contraception is wrong because it goes against the God-given purpose of the sexual faculty or power.

But the teleology of the faculty or power constitutes too limited a perspective and criterion for morality. The faculty exists as part of the person and the person exists in different relationships. A personalistic or relational perspective or criterion comes to a different conclusion. For the good of the person or the good of the person's relationships or the good of the existing children or the good of society in terms of overpopulation, artificial contraception can be justified. One can interfere with the purpose of the faculty for the good of the person or the good of the multiple relationships in which we live. The sexual faculty of a homosexual person differs from the sexual faculty of a heterosexual person. The faculty must always be seen in relationship to the person.

Many Catholic moral theologians apply the same approach to lying. The malice of lying consists in the violation of my neighbor's right to truth — a relational criterion. If my neighbor does not have the right to truth, what I say is a falsehood but not a lie. The person hiding Jews in her home in World War II could answer the Gestapo's question by responding that their were no Jews in her house. Technically speaking this is false speech, but it is not a lie.

Second, a two- or three-layered anthropology also furnishes an inadequate criterion for moral actions. According to Thomistic moral theology human nature has three basic inclinations or tendencies to ends. The first inclination that we share with all living things is to keep ourselves in existence. Thus, human beings can never directly take their own lives because it goes against the basic God-given inclination to keep oneself in existence. Second, human beings share with all animals the inclination to procreation and education of offspring. Thus, human beings can never directly interfere with the sexual faculty and act because that goes against the God-given inclination to procreation. What is proper to human beings is the inclination to live in common and to worship God. One can never directly go against the God-given inclinations to these ends that are proper to human beings. Thus, the human person consists of three layers — what is common to all living things, what is common to human beings and all animals, and what is proper to human beings. But the rational aspect of human beings can never interfere in the animal inclination to procreation even for the good of the person or the person's relationships. The animal and biological processes become sacrosanct and cannot be interfered with.

In this connection, the Catholic natural law tradition accepted the Thomistic understanding or definition of the human being as a rational animal. Note that animal is the noun. The rational part adds something to the animal, but it cannot interfere with or change the animality in any way. Animality, with its biological process, becomes inviolate.

Third, the problem of biologism or physicalism. In the hierarchical Catholic understanding, certain acts described in terms of their physical or biological structure are always and everywhere wrong. Thus, for example, contraception and masturbation are physical acts that are always wrong. For the most part, the Catholic theological tradition has distinguished between the physical and the moral aspects of human acts. Killing is a physical act, but not all killing is wrong. Murder is always wrong, but murder is the moral act of unjustified killing. The physical act is basically what one can take a picture of, but what is physically evil is not necessarily a moral evil. Take the act of slapping another person in the face with some force. This is a physical act. It very often might be a morally bad act of anger or violence or hatred, but it might also be the good act of trying to revive an unconscious person. The problem in the area of sexuality is that we have completely identified the physical aspect of the act with the moral aspect of the act.

Especially in the light of the debate over contraception in the Roman Catholic Church, many people claim that the problem with the hierarchical teaching was its pro-natalist position. The need for procreation was the controlling aspect of the teaching. But such is not the case. Hierarchical Catholic teaching also condemns artificial insemination between spouses even with the husband's semen. Thus, procreation is not the controlling aspect of Catholic hierarchical teaching, because this way of procreating is condemned. The controlling aspect is the physical act of marital intercourse that is always required and can never be interfered with. Physicalism is the problem. The moral act is totally identified with the biological or physical aspect of the act.

The hierarchical teaching insists that these acts described in physical terms are always and everywhere wrong. Contraception, masturbation, and homosexual intercourse can never be justified. They are always and everywhere wrong. I agree that some acts are intrinsically wrong; for example, murder or rape. Such acts are always wrong, but they are moral acts and not physical acts. There exists a problem in maintaining that acts described in physical and not moral terms are intrinsically evil.

The above paragraphs have set out the ecclesial, theological, and ethical contexts for Dr. John E. Perito's remarkable and important book *Contemporary Catholic Sexuality*. John Perito brings to this book his deep knowledge of psychiatry and a lifetime of practice dealing with the issue of sexuality. He does not claim to be a moral theologian, but he offers his understanding of human sexuality based on his profound knowledge and broad experience in the field of psychiatry. In the process, he makes a significant contribution to moral theology and to our understanding of human sexuality.

Perito starts from his dissatisfaction with the position that acts such as contraception, masturbation, and homosexual intercourse are intrinsically evil. The previous paragraphs show why many others, including myself, share this dissatisfaction. The method used by Perito to set forth his own position is very much in keeping with the best of the Catholic theological tradition. The Catholic tradition has insisted that faith and reason can never contradict one another. This is a marvelous affirmation of the importance and significance of human reason. Faith and reason are not opposed. Theology itself has been understood as faith seeking understanding through reason. The Catholic Church sponsored the first universities in the Middle Ages precisely because of the role of reason in discovering truth in all its different dimensions. In its broadest understanding the natural law theory in Catholicism well illustrates this principle that faith and reason cannot contradict one another. Christians, through human reason reflecting on our created humanity, can arrive at moral wisdom and knowledge.

Perito uses his reason and his understanding of human nature and human sexuality to disagree with the concept of human nature that undergirds the hierarchical magisterium's understanding of sexuality. His reason comes from his psychiatric knowledge and experience. Using this basic Catholic methodology, Perito comes to some different conclusions about the meaning of sexuality and its acts.

Dr. Perito also follows the best of Catholic moral methodology in another important aspect of his approach. Too often in the past Catholic moral teaching dealt only with the morality of particular acts — what is often called today quandary ethics. Can I do this or that? Quandary ethics certainly deals with important issues, but quandaries are not all there is to moral theology. At its best the Catholic moral tradition recognized the important questions of moral meaning and the virtues which characterize the moral person. John Perito rightly claims that the most important chapter in his book is the one that deals with spirituality and sexuality. The meaning of sexuality is most significant.

John Perito has not attempted to write the definitive book on sexuality. Many of us will disagree with one or other of his understandings or proposals. But what the Catholic Church badly needs today in the light of the present disarray and crisis in the understanding of human sexuality is to adhere to the best of the Catholic tradition by insisting that faith and reason cannot contradict one another. Unfortunately, the explorations of science informed by faith in the area of sexuality have been curtailed within Roman Catholicism because of authoritative pressure and the result of fears. But the Catholic tradition, especially in times of problems, needs to be faithful to its best theological tradition. *Contemporary Catholic Sexuality* follows in this Catholic tradition and tries to show how reason as found in the theory and practice of psychiatry can help us to better understand the meaning of sexuality. Today the Catholic Church desperately needs an open, broad, and deep dialogue about the meaning of human sexuality. I hope this book encourages such a dialogue on this most important issue.

Charles E. Curran
Elizabeth Scurlock University Professor of
Human Values, Southern Methodist University

Prologue

I first became acquainted with the concept of sexuality about forty years ago during my freshman year in medical school. Learning about sex, of course, occurred much earlier, and I believe even earlier than my parents suspected. Sexuality was introduced in the freshman course on human development. At first the concepts seemed farfetched and not easily understandable. They used terms like "oral," "anal," and "phallic." They told us that sexual feelings begin in infancy and not adolescence as everyone assumes. The Oedipus complex had something to do with a Greek character who fell in love with his mother and killed his father. What did this have to do with our development? Another novel concept was that Freud was not referring to sex when he spoke about sexuality, but simply the experience of pleasure in some part of the body. That still confuses some of us today.

It wasn't until my psychiatric residency, when my wife and I had two children of our own, that the process of psychosexual development began to make some sense. Watching a toddler put everything into her mouth lent some credence to orality, and a two-year-old saying no to everything just to exert power shed some light on anality. I was often amused at the seductiveness of a four-year-old boy in church as he distracted his mother from praying with frequent hugs and kisses, or a little girl of similar age gently stroking her father's face with her fingers.

The expression "Kids say the darndest things" is certainly true when it comes to sex. My five-year-old son was very matter-of-fact when he told me he was going to have two children because he had recently discovered he had two testicles. He thought they were eggs. And my four-year-old daughter gave me a clear sign she was excited about her femininity when she flatly stated that she was "fancy" on the inside because she could make babies.

My real teachers about sexuality, however, were the many patients I treated in psychotherapy and psychoanalysis during thirty years of practice. More than any textbook, they furnished me with material about our marvelous development and the many things that can go wrong with it. The textbook was only a guide; the real material was demonstrated daily as my patients revealed in detail the stories of their lives. I will share some of their stories, in a very disguised form of course, so that others may benefit from their experiences, and mine, as we struggle to understand this very complex part of ourselves we call sexuality.

When I first went into practice, I had the privilege of treating many Roman Catholic priests, religious, and lay people who were attempting to cope with the impact of the Second Vatican Council (1963–65), the worldwide Ecumenical Council of Bishops called by Pope John XXIII, popularly referred to as Vatican II. The church was trying to change, and its members were trying to grow. Many priests and religious brothers and sisters grew completely out of religious life, often with the issue of sexuality at the core of their conflicts. Those who stayed needed to grow through personal recommitment as they viewed the changing attitudes around them. Many people had conflicts over the shift of thinking in sexual ethics, particularly regarding the issue of family planning. Some found conflicts so disturbing that they needed to leave the church, while others found a way to remain by forming a personal conscience differing with official church teaching.

The concept of God's view of sexuality came to me about eight years ago. I too had my growing to do after Vatican II. Coming from a very strict and thorough Catholic education plus four years in the seminary, I was well indoctrinated in Catholic thinking and was looking forward to the changes that Vatican II seemed to promise. In my own struggles for change I found myself more interested in psychiatry and analysis than in religion, and I tended to put much of religion on the shelf. Then one day I took a course entitled "The Spirituality of Everyday Life" given at the Washington Theological Union in Washington, D.C. I assumed it would be an opportunity to get better acquainted with the changes of Vatican II. But its focus was as implied: "The Spirituality of Everyday Life." It allowed me to start thinking more about spirituality than religion. I started seeing "spirituality" as one's life being directed by one's spirit or spiritual force. For Christians "spirituality" includes being guided by the

Holy Spirit. Many of the ideas had to do with psychological concepts which I was quite familiar with pertaining to awareness, living in the here and now, and becoming more friendly with one's body. As I saw the relationship between psychology and spirituality come closer together it had a profound effect on me. I was awakened to the fact that I had been missing something in both fields. The focus of my life shifted and I started pursuing the commonalities in spirituality and psychology. Before too long I was wondering what the Spirit was teaching me about sexuality.

With that shift I realized I had been neglecting a whole dimension in my study of the human mind and heart. I was very comfortable with the biological, psychological, and social aspects of behavior. Now I discovered the fourth dimension, the spiritual one, which before had been buried somewhere in religion. It occurred to me that if spirituality is such a big part of our existence as I had come to appreciate sexuality was, there simply must be a better marriage between the two of them: one I never had been able to appreciate. Putting sexuality and spirituality together had been like trying to mix oil and water. They would never quite blend and would quickly separate again.

It was as if all of my knowledge needed to be examined, only this time in the presence of God. I had spent seven years in personal analysis revealing every imaginable detail of my life to my analyst. It struck me that God had been present in that room at every moment watching me disclose, struggle, and grow. The problem was that I had never acknowledged God's Presence! My focus was on myself and my analyst, but it really needed to be triangular.

In this book I hope to take you on a journey down some of the roads I have traveled as a psychiatrist, psychoanalyst, and practicing believer. We will retrace my steps of listening, reacting to, and trying to understand the journeys shared by many who like myself were in search of meaning, peace, and God in our lives. This time I hope to do it with the illumination of God's Presence. I have become convinced that living in the Presence has a most profound effect on our mental outlook and our lives. Our psychosexual development, our psychology, morality, spirituality, and ethics will be sadly lacking if we are not constantly reflecting upon these subjects in God's Presence.

This book has also been inspired by the developing attitude since Vatican II that lay men and women become more mature in their spirituality by studying Scripture and theology and having dialogue with people of good will. I hope that this book will be seen as a form of dialoguing with all people of good will, within my own tradition as well as with other Christians and other believers and unbelievers.

It is possible for a person to be a mature human being without being Christian. I also believe that it is possible for a person to be a Christian without being a mature human being. Maturity, however, requires some form of spirituality to satisfy the longings of the human heart. Without this meaning we tend to chase after false gods of many different kinds. Extremes of sensual indulgence, including sexual indulgence or abstinence, might very well be indicative of such false gods hiding psychological immaturity and an empty heart.

I am writing this book for those who are interested in the dialogue surrounding the interface between psychology, moral theology, and spirituality. It is for those who see the need for a continued development of sexual ethics. It is also for those who feel there has been too much development already and want to return to pre-Vatican II thinking. I hope that it will not only satisfy Catholics seeking more understanding about sexual matters, but all who seek an integration of sexuality and spirituality in their lives. Much of my writing will have Catholic overtones because of my own background, but because of similar sexual ethics among various denominations and world religions, it may hold an interest for those with an ecumenical and interfaith interest as well. I am becoming more convinced that we need a set of human sexual ethics that can be embraced by all who love themselves and their neighbor, and who perhaps have a sense of God or a Higher Power as well.

I am a psychiatrist and psychoanalyst, not a moral theologian or spiritual director. While I have tried to acquaint myself with the material from those fields as it pertains to sexuality, I do not pretend to be an expert. My interest is in furthering the dialogue, and I welcome criticism from anyone with expertise in those areas.

The *Catechism of the Catholic Church* outlines the authority of the hierarchical structure of the church. It details the role of the pope, the college of bishops in union with him, the authority of an ecumenical council, and the privilege of the laity with regard to the preservation of truth within the church:

In accord with the knowledge, competence, and preeminence which they possess, [lay people] have the right and even at times a duty to manifest to the sacred pastors their opinion on matters which pertain to the good of the Church, and they have a right to make their opinion known to the other Christian faithful, with due regard to the integrity of faith and morals and reverence toward their pastors, and with consideration for the common good and the dignity of persons.[1]

I do not claim preeminence, but because of my knowledge and professional experience I feel some obligation to share it with others.

An infrequent reference to the laity from Vatican II is that the whole body of the faithful "have an anointing that comes from the holy one (1 John 2:20, 27) and cannot err in matters of belief."[2] The document speaks of the role of the laity in matters of evangelization, living out Gospel values in their lives, and bringing their voices and experience and professional expertise to bear on the life of the church.

The church is a "work in the progress." Some teachings are being grasped slowly over time, such as what happened with slavery, while other teachings are consistent, e.g., that Jesus is both God and Man, which has been part of the Catholic faith from the beginning, even if denied by parts of the church in the course of history. Keeping the balance between loyalty to the official teaching and freedom to explore and follow one's conscience is a struggle that has faced believers in every age and especially today.

One of the problems we face is that of trying to appreciate the underlying attitudes that influence our opinions. Scientists are usually willing, but sometimes reluctant, to change ideas and theories as new data arises. This is very difficult for some of us because familiar ideas are comfortable. Some traditionalist Christian believers see themselves with the task of preserving the "Truth" of the past. To them change may be suspect. Others see Tradition as evolving and being created in the present under the guidance of the Spirit. Tradition can easily be trivialized with such Divine Wind in our sails. Certainly all attitudes need to be respected for the truth which they contain. But respect without serious confrontation and challenge leads to stagnation.

The objectives of this book are threefold: (1) to present some theological ideas that pertain to our sexuality, (2) to offer some ideas on sexuality from psychodynamics, the science that studies the workings of the mind and its motivational forces, and (3) to discuss some areas of dialogue between theologians and psychologists regarding sexuality. As the dialogue continues among theologians, psychologists, sociologists, and anthropologists it will deepen our understanding of sexuality and will increase our ability to foster proper development and integration of sexuality to the enrichment of the person and the common good.

As a psychoanalyst who embraces many of Freud's teachings, I will naturally be presenting ideas that I know others might disagree with or see as outdated. My experience has convinced me of the validity of the observations that I am presenting. I also believe that there is no universal psychological theory of human behavior. Often the contributions of several theories taken together, particularly when they do not contradict one another, can give us a fuller picture of truth. Setting theories aside, I personally have come to believe that when we really love someone from the core of our being, our basic desire is to do them no harm. That aspect of sexuality will govern our sexual acts.

As a practicing Christian, I am assuming the sacredness of human life, the special creation of the human person "in God's image and likeness" (Gen. 1:26), and the eternal destiny of humans. God calls us into friendship. All human experience and conduct is governed by these faith-informed principles. Sexuality then is a noble gift with an eternal purpose.

The examples I use are meant to illustrate clinical issues, but they have been disguised so as to prevent any connection with particular individuals. They are sometimes composites of more than one case for the purpose of illustration as well as disguise. They have been written in the chapter in which they demonstrate some of the features being discussed, but upon reflection it will be easy to see that they might just as easily have been placed in another chapter. This is significant because it shows just how complex we are and how difficult it is to examine one clinical situation without consideration of several others. Any similarity to names of real persons is purely coincidental because I have randomly selected names and used them in alphabetical order.

Acknowledgments

No one writes a book without the help of many others. I would like to express my deepest gratitude to all who have shared their stories with me and to the many colleagues who have read various drafts of this work and contributed greatly to its content and organization. This work would not have been possible without their dialogue with me.

I would particularly like to thank Father Frank Kinny of the Walter Reed Army Medical Center, who first suggested that I could write a book; Father Kevin O'Neil of the Washington Theological Union for his courses in moral theology and sexual ethics, which provided a broad study of moral issues; my brother-in-law and psychiatric colleague, Dr. Louis Conte, for helping me with the early conceptualization and initiation of this work; Father Charles Curran of Southern Methodist University for his foreword, manuscript review, and encouragement to seek publication when it was difficult; Father Miles Riley, whose philosophy of telling the truth with kindness I hope had some influence; Paul Hendrickson, who provided the model of an author and encouraged me to become one; Father Stephen Rossetti for sharing ideas on pedophilia; my editors, Hugh Behan and Mary C. Connor-Spieler, for their help in continually pressing me for clarity of thought and expression of ideas, and Alison Donohue, Paul McMahon, and Roy M. Carlisle, editors at The Crossroad Publishing Company, for selecting my work for publication and seeing it through to completion. I am very grateful to Roy Carlisle, who showed me, as we moved through the final draft, the excitement of precise expression. When I felt the final draft was almost completed, his attitude was similar to an analyst's with patients who have just poured out their heart: "Now we can begin."

I wish to recognize my wife, Pat, for her editorial work and patience with the time and preoccupation writing this book has taken.

I feel a particular debt of gratitude to my analyst, the late Dr. Paul Gray, for his patience, wisdom, and assistance in enriching my personal and professional life. Dr. Gray pioneered the idea in psychoanalysis of intrapsychic viewing in the here and now. His ideas resonate throughout this book.

I would like to thank members of the staff of the Shalem Institute for Spiritual Formation for the programs that I had the opportunity to attend, particularly Dr. Jerry May, who first encouraged my writing and reviewed early manuscripts, and Barbara Osborne, who opened the door between psychology and spirituality for me.

My nephew, Bill Kahl, deserves special mention for his constant availability with computer help to keep the project moving.

Finally I would like to thank God for the graces of being able to envision and complete this work on a topic that deals so much with the very spark of our existence.

I take full responsibility for all the ideas expressed within these pages and do not suggest that they are endorsed by anyone with whom I have had the privilege of discussion.

CONTEMPORARY
CATHOLIC
SEXUALITY

Part I

Basics

Chapter 1

Introduction

Sexual ethics in the Catholic Church are in a state of flux. Vatican II brought some changes in the way marriage is viewed by considering procreation and mutual love between spouses to have equal value. But the underlying sexual ethical principles were to remain the same. Various theologians now view sexual behaviors differently as do a large number of Catholics. While welcoming the equality of procreation in marriage and the mutual love between spouses, they feel that it is imperative to challenge the underlying sexual principles which can make achieving both ends difficult or impossible for many of us. Dialogue about basic sexual principles and relational issues is the purpose of this book, supported by a discussion of sexuality in general.

The United States Catholic bishops published a document entitled *Human Sexuality: A Catholic Perspective for Education and Lifelong Learning,*[3] in which they define sexuality as "a fundamental component of personality in and through which we, as male or female, experience our relatedness to self, others, the world, and even God."

I agree with this definition and tend to qualify it further. I think of sexuality as referring to the energy involved in our relatedness. It is only in the more narrow sense that it refers to our capacity to participate together with God's power in the wonder of procreation through love. Sexuality is a special gift and mystery which we continually strive to understand. In its broader sense it includes the way we relate to the world as male or female, that is, according to gender. It encompasses all the attitudes, feelings, and behaviors of relating. It includes the attractions or aversions that we feel toward each other. We relate through our bodies and our senses, our hearts and our minds. Genitality is obviously included in sexuality as is sexual orientation. Sexuality is strongly affected

29

by the culture of our society and religious upbringing as experienced in the family and school.

Joan Timmerman describes sexuality in *Sexuality and Spiritual Growth* as the "entire range of feelings and behaviors which human beings have and use as embodied persons in the world, expressing relationship to themselves and others through look, touch, word, and action. It includes the combination of our gender (identity and role) and sex (anatomy and physiology) and is coextensive with personality."[4]

Psychoanalysts usually describe sexuality as having two instinctual components: a sexual drive and an aggressive drive. The sexual drive has to do with our striving for a variety of pleasures and satisfactions that promote our survival and well-being, while the aggressive drive is the assertive principle assisting in the pursuit of these needs. If we examine behaviors closely it is easy enough to see the two drives acting in unison. Both are necessary. The Spanish have a saying: the baby who does not cry will not suck. The act of sucking itself has its aggressive component as the infant vigorously draws on the breast to obtain nourishing and satisfying milk.

Part of the mystery of our sexuality is that *God does not give it to us all at once, nor does God give us our personal or scientific understanding of it all at once.* They are imparted to us in stages through our experience and psychosexual development as well as through our scientific and theological investigations.

I feel it is important that this gift of sexuality be understood with an awareness of God's role in designing it and in sustaining our existence through each developmental stage. We go through a development that is marvelously crafted, one stage building upon another, from our first awareness of body parts to our adult acts of intimacy and intercourse. Lack of appreciation for this might lead us to denigrate our bodies in favor of our minds, failing to integrate the many factors that go into our psychosexual development and undermining our God-given human sacredness.

God has designed a human sexual responsiveness which is very complex. This responsiveness is not something that two people should expect to find miraculously established when they go before the altar and pronounce wedding vows. Neither can it be ignored once one has taken a vow of celibacy. Nor is its maturation achieved with serial partners offering little more than sexual pleasure. Individuals with such expectations will often end up in therapists' offices, in divorce courts, or before church tribunals asking for an annulment or seeking release from their celibacy vows.

God was very imaginative in giving sexual powers to humans and animals so that reproduction would come through relatedness. Animal and human behavior in terms of sexuality, mating, and reproduction is similar in many ways though there are some key differences. Humans and animals both nurture and protect their young. Animals share our need for care and, and in many instances, love. The development in humans of a thinking capacity, a sense of morality, and the powers of reflection contributed to our "psychosexual" development. These qualities brought into existence certain differences in the ways humans relate as opposed to animals. And I must say it is not always for the better. It takes years of psychosexual and social development for humans to acquire a capacity to participate fully in God's plan for procreation and to be able to sustain an intimate sexual relationship. A national divorce rate of over 50 percent tells us how difficult it is to select a proper partner and keep a lifelong commitment. Even the experimental living together which is so popular today has done nothing to affect this divorce rate. Maybe we have come to expect more from marriage than our parents did. Have we come to expect too much?

Human sexual responsiveness can miscarry in many ways. There are those who avoid relationships where the possibility of sexual excitement might arise. This is not a matter of choice because the sexual relationship might be inappropriate. It is from a fear of intimacy for a variety of reasons which will be discussed further. That intimacy may be psychological as well as physical. There are those very dependent individuals frightened by authority figures who worry about how the authority figures might regard their sexual expressions. Many individuals have fears of sexual desire or inhibitions of intercourse which are often unclear but still very real. There are a variety of sexual addictions that can consumes one's life. And there are many sexual perversions occurring when there has been serious disruption in the developmental process.

In order to understand and appreciate these many difficulties, it is necessary for parents, teachers, and other social leaders to be attuned to the complexities of psychosexual development, as well as to many other social and cultural factors that affect maturation.

When I was in the seminary before Vatican II there was no such concept as "dialogue," except of course in the ordinary sense of the word. We were taught Thomistic philosophy and theology in great detail. There was a course in the history of philosophy, but very little about other schools of theology. The Thomistic view was considered to be the "truth" sufficient for our own understanding and adequate to prepare us to argue intelligently with whomever we might encounter.

Non-Thomistic psychology was suspect because of its strong Freudian influence. Freud was suspect because of his atheistic point of view and because of his emphasis on sexuality, which was very poorly understand by many. Scientists were suspect because they focused on what is observable and validated, and they had no room for faith. Most were considered atheists or agnostics which could have been true then, but studies today show that at least 40 percent of scientists are people of faith. Other religions and spiritualities were suspect because they were not part of the one true faith and therefore in need of conversion.

Today Catholics have an attitude that exchanging ideas respectfully with people of other religions and spiritualities and with scientists is a valuable thing and in fact the only way to arrive at truth. One hopes the naiveté, ignorance, and arrogance of the past will not return.

Chapter 2

Theology, Psychology, and Sexuality

God's view of sexuality is a subject that has preoccupied Christians and theologians covertly or overtly from the earliest of times. One of the church's earliest sexual issues arose at the time of St. Paul. At one stage of his ministry he believed that the coming of the Savior was imminent. Paul therefore encouraged the early Christians not to marry and to abstain from sexual intercourse in preparation for salvation. Given the nearness of the Second Coming as perceived by Paul and the first generation of Christians, there was no need to think about procreation.

There was another early sexual issue involving celibacy and salvation. The early Christians believed that a sure way to salvation was by martyrdom. After the executions of Christians ceased, some Christians began to seek a kind of martyrdom through self-sacrifice. One avenue of self-sacrifice was the practice of celibacy, later called "white martyrdom." It would seem that these early attitudes played their part in establishing the ideal that the sexual celibate life was preferable to marriage and sexual intercourse for those who aspired to holiness.

St. Augustine (354–430 A.D.), bishop of Hippo in North Africa, was very influential in the development of sexual ethics. Even after his Christian conversion, he was influenced by the philosophy of Manicheanism, which taught dualism in claiming that the spirit is good and matter is evil. St. Augustine taught that married couples should not take pleasure in sexual intercourse. He said that although sexual acts are necessary for procreation, taking pleasure in them is at least venially sinful. This teaching remained until the thirteenth century, when St. Thomas Aquinas proposed that sexual pleasure was permissible in marriage and not

33

sinful, but was only secondary to the primary purpose of marriage, the procreation of children.

St. Thomas was the very explicit in trying to understand God's view of sexuality when he developed his natural law theory. He saw natural law as a manifestation of divine law or eternal law, which exists in the mind of the God. He felt it was possible to understand what the Creator had in mind by studying the nature of his creatures. It might be analogous to examining the structure and function of a machine very carefully in order to get some idea of the blueprint in the mind of the designing engineer. This type of thinking has formed the real backbone of sexual ethics, which strongly informs the church's teachings to this day.

Richard Gula, a moral theologian and seminary professor, in *Reason Informed by Faith*, had this to say about St. Thomas and the natural law tradition:

> The natural law is central to Roman Catholic moral theology. It is the kind of "reasoning" which "faith" informs. Perhaps the single most characteristic feature of traditional Catholic morality is that the Church can teach a morality which is applicable always, everywhere, and for everyone because it relies on the natural law as the basis for its teaching. In fact, the claim of the Roman Catholic natural law tradition is that moral knowledge is accessible not just to believers but to anyone who is willing to reflect critically on human experience. The advantage of using natural law is that the Church shows great respect for human goodness and trusts the human capacity to know and choose what is right.[5]

Some of us will immediately react by thinking that the church does not have a morality which is applicable always, everywhere, and for everyone, because when it comes to sexual ethics there is not sufficient consideration of human experience, and some of the arguments from natural law are anything but convincing. But Gula continues:

> By the high Middle Ages there were two strains of interpretation that dominated the natural law tradition. One, "the order of nature," identified with the Stoics and Ulpian, focused on the physical and biological structures given in nature as the source of

morality. The other, "the order of reason," identified with Aristotle, Cicero, and Gaius, focused on the human capacity to discover and experience what benefits human beings. St. Thomas accepted both. Since his teaching is the seminal influence on the traditional Catholic use of natural law, subsequent Catholic theology has been influenced by both interpretations as well.[6]

When St. Thomas considered sexual matters, however, he focused more on the "order of nature" than on the "order of reason," leading to a much more restricted view in considering sexual ethics. It led to his proposing that an action is intrinsically evil when it is opposed to nature, that is, when it frustrates the natural purpose of a faculty or a particular ability to do something. For example, the faculty for speech is to communicate truth. Therefore, lying is intrinsically wrong. The sexual faculties are for procreation. Therefore, any use of these faculties that is not for reproduction is intrinsically evil. Specifically, sexual acts that are performed without the male semen being placed in the female vagina are intrinsically evil. Other examples of intrinsically evil acts are masturbation, contraception, and homosexual acts. Many important aspects of human sexuality are thereby excluded because the notion of intrinsic evil automatically discards them. Such important considerations as the intention of the person performing the action, or the circumstances which might surround the action, are not capable of redeeming an action that is considered intrinsically evil. That is precisely the meaning of the word "intrinsic." Circumstances, intention, and awareness might alter personal subjective responsibility, but the action would still be considered objectively wrong in all circumstances.

The faculties of intellect and will have the purposes of seeking truth and making judgments and choices based upon reasoning. We can argue then that it is intrinsically evil not to use the order of reason in establishing all of natural law, including sexual ethics. It follows that it is intrinsically evil not to freely make individual moral choices in conscience formation. Therefore we can see that there are inherent contradictions in the "intrinsic evil" line of reasoning.

Gula is also helpful when it comes to understanding the "order of reason":

An accurate appeal to this classic understanding of natural law, then, depends on discovering what being "human" really means. This is the work of reason reflecting on the totality of human experience and not only one aspect of it, such as the physical or biological. Reason is not to be construed here in the narrow sense of logic or analysis. Reason, in the Thomistic sense of *recta ratio*, right reason, entails the totality of the human tendency to want to know the whole of reality and come to truth. This sense of reason includes observation and research, intuition, affection, common sense, and an aesthetic sense in an effort to know human reality in all its aspects. In short, whatever resources we can use to understand the meaning of being human will be appropriate for the natural law approach to morality.[7]

Gula continues:

This fundamental understanding of natural law shows St. Thomas' preference for the rational aspects of natural law, a view hardly reconcilable with the biological natural law of Ulpian's definition. If St. Thomas were consistent, the case against Ulpian's definition would then be closed and the Catholic tradition of natural law might well have followed the "order of reason" interpretation throughout its moral teaching.[8]

And finally, Gula states:

The trend in Roman Catholic moral theology today is to develop more and more the rational aspects of the natural law tradition. In this use, reason, and not the physical structure of human faculties or actions taken by themselves, becomes the standard of natural law.[9]

It must be stated that, while this may be the trend in Catholic morality today, it has not been reflected in official Catholic church teaching regarding sexual ethics.

A similar view of "natural law" is expressed by Lisa Cahill, a professor of moral theology at Boston College, in her booklet *Women and Sexuality:*

The Roman Catholic tradition is particularly hospitable to the assumption that investigation of human experience will contribute fruitfully to normative ethics. The approach implied by the term "natural law" validates the appropriateness of the experiential criterion in the discovery of moral truth. Natural law morality is based precisely on theories about human experience, theories derived from basic and shared human realities such as life, sex, and society.[10]

St. Thomas may have felt the need to emphasize the "order of nature" over the "order of reason" because he was influenced by faulty biology. At that time the whole human being was considered to be contained in the male semen. The female was more or less considered as an incubator that allowed the fetus to develop. With these premises in mind, it is easy to understand how an ejaculation not deposited in the female vagina would be viewed as murder or manslaughter. Morality was so strongly determined by the nature of the act itself that even rape and incest were considered less evil than masturbation and deliberately interrupted intercourse because rape and incest were considered natural acts. (Apparently the prevailing Thomistic notion that the soul was not infused into the male body until the fifth month and into the female body until the seventh month was not brought up in this context.)

Major ethical development has been occurring in philosophical and, by extension, theological thinking since Vatican II. One change was termed a shift from "physicalism" to "personalism," referring to a fundamental change from an *action-centered* to a *person-centered* approach in determining what is right or wrong. Now, in appraising the morality of an action, the person is to be considered in relation to self, others, the world, and God while the action becomes just part of the picture. It seems also to have been a shift away from the "order of nature" to the "order of reason." This has had particular application when it comes to developing sexual ethics.

This new point of view in my opinion truly sets the stage for dialogue between theology and psychology. As a result of this shift, theologians and psychologists are essentially studying the same subject, namely, *the human person in relationship,* even if from a different viewpoint. This newer approach also echoes St. Thomas and his *recta ratio* view of natural law, namely, the human tendency to want to know the whole of reality and the reliance in part on observation, experience, or research into actual human behavior to accomplish this.

Clearly there are areas of common interest between theology and psychology, and each discipline has a need for the other. Psychology without theology can leave out our spiritual side and its yearning for meaning for our existence. Theology without psychology would leave us without an understanding of the substrate upon which grace needs to operate. Failure to provide this understanding can lead to considerable pain when natural forces are not taken into consideration in pursuit of our spiritual desires.

We humans have thought patterns that are most difficult to alter once they are established. As a church, we are not in any hurry to change our beliefs. But changes we do make. It took seven hundred years between the time of St. Augustine and the time of St. Thomas before there was any authoritative teaching that sexual pleasure in marriage is not a sin. It took another seven hundred years before the secondary end of marriage, the mutual love and support for the spouses, was placed on a par with the primary end, namely, the procreation and education of children. (This happened at Vatican II.) When the church does change directions on something, it is more like the turn of an ocean liner than a speed boat.

Slavery was accepted as morally permissible for centuries, but now is considered immoral. Prejudice has always been considered against justice and charity, but prejudice against women is still alive and well. Galileo was silenced because he taught that the sun and not the earth was the center of the universe, because the Bible said the "sun stopped in the sky" (Josh. 10:13). He was later exonerated by the findings of science.

Two key figures in the dialogue between theology and psychology are St. Thomas and Sigmund Freud. Both were psychologists. Both observed human beings and were interested in psychological functioning and in constructing theories to explain their observations. St. Thomas in the thirteenth century had neither the psychological microscope (the analytic method) nor the physical microscope that were available to Freud in the twentieth century. Obviously this would make a difference in what they were able to observe. Given that there were different observations, there would also be different theories. How they each, as theologian and nonbeliever, might have been influenced in their findings is hard to say.

All that any of us can go on are the tools and abilities we have at hand. Only God has the overall eternal perspective.

When it comes to our sexuality there are many possible topics for dialogue between theology and psychology. Sexuality is God's gift to us and it comes in various forms and intensities throughout our entire lives. I would like to consider several areas of sexuality that have significant psychological and ethical impact. Obviously the topics that I have chosen are far from exhaustive, but they seem to be the major areas that come up in conversations when the issues of sexuality and ethics are discussed.

Fundamental to all of these topics is the issue of talking about sex and sexuality. One is often treated as though it were the other. Obviously the word "dialogue" implies an equal two-way conversation. But when it comes to a conversation about these issues, it is often fraught with many difficulties and stymied by silences. These difficulties can arise whether we are talking about scientific investigation or personal revelation. Sex is rightfully considered a private matter, and both speaker and listener need to be respectful of that. Sexuality is frequently tarnished with the same brush as sex, so consequently either subject can become taboo. St. Ignatius, who was the founder of the Society of Jesus, told his followers that their chastity was to be like the angels; St. Benedict, who was the founder of a monastic community that involved a vow of celibacy, had nothing to say on the subject. Some parents will hold off talking about sex with their children until there is some crisis or until they finally decide their children are ready to listen respectfully to knowledge that has already been acquired elsewhere (and, not infrequently, falsely, with "dirty" or inaccurate connotations).

When we do talk about sex, we will often struggle with feelings of shame or guilt about sexual behaviors or fantasies. We frequently fear that the listener will think ill or be judgmental about what is being said. In spite of these stumbling blocks there is the need to speak about these issues, for scientific advancement as well as for personal clarification, education, reassurance, direction, and many times for the purpose of relieving an emotional or moral burden of guilt that has been carried for many years.

The listener can do no better than to present an attitude of compassion and openness. This requires of the listener a certain degree of comfort with his or her own sexuality. We need to be able to handle our own very natural voyeuristic impulses that arise in such a discussion and not let them interfere with whatever understanding we are seeking. If we allow our listening to be disrupted because we start to get too curious sexually and lose sight of the fact that we are trying to understand and not indulge some prurient interest, we can easily do a disservice to ourselves and the person trying to communicate with us. Sometimes, we need to be respectful of the reluctance to talk about sex and be willing to encourage, to whatever degree is necessary, the speaker to feel free and know that he or she will be taken seriously.

There is true benefit and growth to be gained in revealing this very private part of ourselves to the right listener. If we are not able to speak about the sexual matters that trouble us, we are more prone to anxiety and confusion than if we were to reveal them and deal with them more consciously. It is a well-accepted concept in psychology that what we do not own will own us: that is, by repression behaviors will come from our unconscious. "The truth shall make you free" (John 8:32) is a sound psychological and mental health principle.

Freud is often falsely accused of being a determinist and denying the existence of free will because he was trying to demonstrate the strong influence which the unconscious has on behaviors. It is referred to as psychic determinism. When Freud was teaching that we can be motivated by factors coming from the unconscious and therefore out of our control, he was not denying free will: he was only denying free will or free choice over what was unknown. Thomists hold the same view when they describe the will as a blind faculty. Without knowledge there can be no choice. Freud saw human freedom as dependent upon making unconscious forces conscious. Talking is our biggest asset to that end.

Given the changes that have transpired since the time of St. Thomas, I wonder if we are now in a position to appreciate some different ideas in our approach to God's view of sexuality — and to say that modern psychology can be included. I will attempt to develop this in more detail in the next chapter.

Chapter 3

Psychodynamics
and Sexuality

Freud needs to be given credit for initiating our psychodynamic view of the human mind and our psychosexual theories of development. He discovered that some of these operations occur outside of our personal awareness. His psychoanalytic method of observation brought to psychology what the microscope brought to the science of medicine. It allows us to see the detailed workings of the mind as never before. The application of psychoanalytic principles to various therapies has not only provided therapeutic benefits, but has enhanced our understanding of personality development and a variety of psychological disorders. One aspect of personality development is psychosexual development, which occurs in stages. God created us in such a way that our human development, including sexuality and all that it implies, comes in increments. Psychologists merely try to observe, understand, and describe it by applying the concept of stages.

The principle that "grace builds on nature" is frequently referred to in philosophy and theology. What I will be proposing here is that we have a chance to appreciate nature as God created it in us by watching how we develop psychosexually. It will be clear that although some things might be explainable by environmental or cultural influences, there are many things that are given to us by God directly. We did not create them. God did, and we can see a great deal of what God intended our development to be by studying these givens. I will endeavor in each section to describe something of what I consider these givens to be. Once we can see what is good for the development of these givens, there will be a foundation on which to judge what is morally and spiritually good. We will be able to see how the grace of God may enter into their operation and development.

This will be in contrast to considering nature from an abstract philosophical system. Granted, it has some data upon which to build these abstractions; nevertheless, it does not provide the data that has been obtained through psychoanalytic investigation.

A personal vignette might help to illustrate just how early these psychosexual stages of development begin. When I had the privilege of holding a new granddaughter for the first time, she soon began to fuss. My son suggested that I let her suck on my little finger while he located her mother, who was capable of responding to her real need. I was amazed at the force and energy with which the infant began sucking.

A while later, after she had been properly nursed, I was holding her again. This time she was content and peaceful. While she was in my lap I cradled her little head in my hand. It seemed to fit perfectly. She made no effort to move for a long time. Needless to say, neither did I. For me, it was a truly spiritual moment. I thought of biblical phrases, such as "I have carved you on the palm of my hand," and "I knitted you while you were in your mother's womb." I felt for a moment that I could glimpse God's love for us, through my love for her. I knew that, no matter what, I would love her all my life. She was less than one month old, and her psychosexual development was well under way. She clearly felt what it meant to be hungry for food and in need of holding. She sensed what it meant to be cuddled and consoled. She experienced physical intimacy and so did I.

Psychosexual development is psychological development closely intertwined with sexual development. The inclusiveness of each of those ideas, *psychological and sexual*, will become clear as we examine the various stages. Normal development occurs in a sequence of various stages with different parts of the body having erotic or pleasurable experiences at different ages. The stages are named according to the part of the body that is the predominant focus of attention. I have predominantly used Freud's concepts from *Three Essays on the Theory of Sexuality* and Erikson's concepts from *Childhood and Society* in developing these stages.[11] Each stage begins with a psychodynamic description and is followed by what I would consider some theological integration.

The first, or oral, stage is the most basic and most important because life itself depends upon what happens during this stage, and all of the other stages are built upon it. Subsequent development will depend upon how successful has been the passage through this oral stage. It occurs between birth and eighteen months. A mother feeding her baby is providing not only nourishment but love, affection, and the opportunity for psychological attachment that will be the foundation for all future relationships. As the mother invests in the baby, the baby invests in the mother. The baby develops a basic trust that mother, or a mothering figure, will be available for food, relief of tension that occurs because of being cold or wet, and comfort by holding, rocking, hugging, and initiating human responsiveness. The hours we spend smiling at, feeding, cleaning, encouraging, cuddling, enjoying, and stimulating our infants with a variety of human touches as well as objects and toys are all basic to psychological and physical well-being. According to Erikson, when this does not happen, a basic distrust is established that will likewise affect future relationships.

During this first year of life, as mother performs her many caretaking duties, she stimulates all sorts of pleasurable sensations which the infant then seeks to reproduce. Infants are often observed putting a variety of objects into their mouths. Renee Spitz, a developmental psychologist, has made some valuable observations about early infant care. One is that infants who are only fed and are not stimulated or responded to with loving attention are at risk of actually dying. Another is that during the first year of life, when the relationship between mother and infant is what it should be in many different ways, the infant develops more rapidly and genital play is more frequent. When the relationship is disturbed, development is slower and genital play is rare, or other autoerotic activities replace it, such as rocking or head banging. If these autoerotic activities are not recognized as the infant's cry for help, he or she will become lethargic and sink into what appears to be a kind of depression.[12]

Recently a new diagnostic category has been established and labeled "detachment disorder." It occurs in infants who have had sufficient physical nourishment and shelter to survive but have not been loved, in an unconditional and emotional way. The essential bonding that should occur during this stage is lacking. These infants have not been loved

and consequently they have failed to develop the capacity to reciprocate. They show no desire to please a loving parent because there was
no loving parent present for them. The trade-off of love for appropriate
behavior does not occur. We very much use the desire to please our parents as a motive to learn appropriate behaviors. Doing the right thing
brings praise and affection. If praise and affection are not given freely
and spontaneously to the infant, the need for them is not consciously
experienced. Consequently the trade-off of love for appropriate behavior is not possible. These children will then be essentially unmanageable.
They do not seem to care about themselves or others. They will hurt
themselves and/or others and often seem unreachable. The children who
have been taken into foster homes with this condition become a terrific
challenge to their foster or adopting parents. Many times they are so
unmanageable that they have to be given up. Those that can be helped
need to learn the meaning of unconditional love first if they are to be
helped.

Theological integration

God created our mouths and our oral drives. God also created our minds
and hearts so that what happens to us physiologically during this stage
will also determine what happens to us psychologically. An infant who
is open to mother's love and is satisfied and secure can become open to
the world. The oral drives have to do with consuming in many ways:
food, satisfaction, love, security, beauty, excitement. I love to watch my
granddaughters at this stage. Everything goes into their mouths. They
put their fingers into our mouths. They finger our faces, eyes, and ears,
and I have the special privilege of getting my beard pulled. We were
meant to take in. This openness of attitude can be easily transferred
to the eyes as the infant absorbs its world with many new and curious
objects at every turn. This is the way that God made us. The divine plan
was for us to consume life, with all that the word "consume" implies.
We were made to frequently nourish our bodies and also our souls.
Christ provided the sacrament of communion as our oral avenue to the
divine. We were made to take in the universe and marvel at its awesome
components. We have been instructed to "hunger and thirst for justice"
and we will be filled (Matt. 5, the Beatitudes). Our minds and hearts
were meant to devour as we go through life, advancing in wisdom and

age and grace. We are to take in the Spirit with our breath and allow the Divine Presence to permeate our beings. *God unconditionally loves us and simply wants us to love ourselves and each other.*

In the second, or anal, stage of development, the anus is the organ of erotic attention. Holding on or letting go, namely, control, is the fundamental developmental issue. It occurs between eighteen months and three years. Other issues include pleasing or struggling with parents, autonomy, body ownership, cleanliness, and orderliness. Each one of these issues of course has profound psychological implications.

Control and who has it is a lifelong psychological issue. It starts here with toilet training and the need for children to gain bowel and bladder control. Parents need to recognize that this is an issue and sometimes a battle that they cannot get into because they will lose. Children learn and hopefully come to appreciate that they are the ones with the power to control their own bodies and by so doing can please or displease parents. There is a kind of pleasure in learn how to hold on and let go of feces and urine that becomes the central focus in control. If a child chooses to release at an inopportune moment because it will feel good, there can be parental disapproval. Likewise, doing so when they get to the bathroom will bring parental approval and praise. Parents need to make sure that children are physiologically capable of control before they try to impose it. Otherwise the child cannot please parents at the sacrifice of some delay in the pleasure of discharge. This problem will lead not only to a much longer and painful period of toilet training, but frequently to struggles with control in other areas of life and not infrequently to personality difficulties.

The early seed of autonomy grows into freedom and independence. Considerable pleasure and happiness in life come from this sense of freedom in many areas. It is one of the most highly prized possessions in our way of life. Guaranteed by the Constitution and fought for in many wars, personal freedom is a right Americans hold dear. There are mini-wars in families where this very basic human need is not respected and helped along in its development. When children are too dominated or controlled, they may be contained or managed for a while, but it usually will not last; some form of rebellion will occur, often with severe consequences to the children and their families.

We all need to own our own bodies, respect them and care for them. Without this body appreciation we will not be inclined to care for our health and by extension may be less careful with the bodies of others. Again the basic process of the attitudes that we establish about our bodies and the way our needs were satisfied during a particular developmental phase will become the attitudes that we establish toward our minds. Keeping feces and expelling them becomes the template for keeping or expelling many other things. Some of us play everything "close to the vest." Some of us can be "read like an open book." Some of us are always "spilling our guts" and some of us are "tight asses." We use the phrase "anal-retentive."

The sense of not being able to control the body might lead to a sense of not being able to control our mind or our thoughts and feelings. The feeling that our body is dirty can be a precursor to the feeling that our mind is dirty. This happens by a simple process called displacement, a mental mechanism that shifts an affect or feeling from one object to another. Genital touching may now be associated with something mother says is dirty, shameful, and not to be done, such as touching feces. This displacement can contribute to many sexual difficulties later in life, such as impotence, vaganismus, and difficulty with orgasm.

Cleanliness and orderliness can be a blessing or a curse. We obviously need cleanliness for health, and being a clean person is a value in our culture. Having things in a proper place will lead to accomplishments that cannot be achieved with things in a state of disarray. When we become preoccupied with neatness and orderliness they can actually interfere with more important tasks in life. One of my patients was so preoccupied with the order of his desk that he had trouble doing his work. Another was so fearful of picking up germs she could not touch things in a grocery store or a department store if she saw someone had just touched the product she was interested in. Another patient would wipe off silverware and glassware that she had not personally washed. This had to be done very surreptitiously when she was at a dinner party.

We sometimes hear of the anal-retentive character. These are persons who always have to be in control or have to hang on to everything. They will be reluctant to make commitments until the very last minute in order to keep the options open for something better to come along. They will frequently turn the conversation to what interests them and grudgingly listen until the opportunity for them to speak again can be created. It can be manifested in someone who seldom shows ideas, someone who is stingy or tight and lives for isolative internal pleasure.

Theological integration

God created our bowels and our anal drives. God wishes us to be in control of our lives. He desires us to make choices and be responsible for those we make. God's desire for our freedom is as great as our own. Our freedom is so respected that we are allowed to sin, to choose creatures over the Creator and to fill ourselves with emptiness instead of divine grace. We can give generously of ourselves to others, or we can share nothing of ourselves with others. We can control and dominate others, or we can seek their growth, independence, and freedom. We can shame ourselves or others, and we can bless ourselves and others. *God unconditionally love us and simply wants us to love ourselves and each other.*

In the third, or genital, stage of development the genitals are the organs of interest and pleasure. This stage occurs between three and six years of age. This is the age of curiosity about one's own genitals and those of others. "Playing doctor" is a way that children legitimize their curiosity, and the process helps them to differentiate between the sexes. Children soon learn that this must be done secretly because of parental disapproval. If there is sufficient psychosexual development up to this point, masturbation, orgasm, and sexual fantasies do occur. (A fantasy is a mental image or picture with assorted feelings. For example, a child may picture a mother with a loving breast and answering every need, or a father who is larger than life, very scary and threatening.) Masturbation is more deliberate than the genital rubbing which occurred during the oral and anal phases. An orgasm, if it occurs, is a release of sexual tension, which in the male at this age is without ejaculation. Ejaculation occurs only with pubertal sperm formation. The fantasies of this period may have many different qualities. They may be positive-oedipal, that is, referring to the little boy's physical attraction toward his mother or the little girl's physical attraction toward her father. They may be negative-oedipal, that is, referring to the little boy's physical attraction toward his father and the little girl's physical attraction toward her mother. These fantasies may involve looking, touching, showing, kissing, undressing — all with a quality of sexual excitement. These are the precursors of the fantasies of adolescence which it is hoped will bring the individual to a realistic understanding of what full sexual intercourse is all about as part of an intimate relationship in later married life.

As a little illustration of a four-year-old's sexual interest, I offer the following story. A little boy approached his mother with the following question: "Mommy, do you like big penises or little penises better?" After a swallow and a pause, she answered with the wisdom of Solomon. "I like big penises on big boys, and little penises on little boys." With that answer he seemed satisfied and returned to playing.

Theological integration

God created our genitals and as such declared us partners in creation. He wanted us to be male and female, masculine and feminine, with the latter two terms referring to all of the inherently different qualities that we possess as male and female. We tend to kid these days about such and such being a "guy" thing or such and such being a "girl" thing, but there are inherently different attitudes that can be seen in very early child play that speak to this difference. In general, boys like to play with guns and trucks. In general, girls like to play with dolls and tea sets. However, both girls and boys are capable of learning science and math, literature and art, sports and physical conditioning. And the big difference these days is that both women and men are viewed as capable of child rearing, and many do share in the responsibility.

God gave us pleasure in these genital organs from birth on through life that we might discover and enjoy that pleasure. What starts as self-pleasure extends to pleasure with another. We have intense curiosities about each other as male and female, which can lead to informing each other of our differences as well as our similarities. God created us equally important in the area of reproduction, but the roles are obviously quite different. The male impregnates and the female is impregnated. We have had the irrational fantasy that the man is "superior" because he is active and penetrating, and the female is "inferior" because she is passive or receptive. Unfortunately those ideas have been incorrectly assumed and philosophized and theologized for centuries. As a result the development of both sexes has been affected negatively.

It is one of the most exciting and valuable accomplishments of our age that these notions has been challenged. Of course, I do not bring any prejudice myself to this position as the grandfather of three beautiful and talented granddaughters! They will be raised, as will many young girls of today, in such a way as not to bring any inferiority to the banquet of life. And, if I have anything to say about it, the environment which fosters such inferiority and superiority attitudes will be changed as well.

The Vatican's Pontifical Council for the Family, in a document entitled "The Truth and Meaning of Human Sexuality," has this to say: "From the earliest age, parents may observe the beginning of instinctive genital activity in their child. It should not be considered repressive to correct such habits gently that could become sinful later and, when necessary, to teach modesty as the child grows."[13]

I would respectfully beg to differ that it should be considered repressive and therefore unhealthy for the following reasons. As stated earlier, genital play is a positive sign that there is healthy bonding and interchange between the mother and child. Genital play is a way for infants to discover their bodies; by touch and genital pleasure they begin to feel positively about their bodies and themselves. It is part of self-discovering, self-comforting, self-ownership, and self-identity. It is only after we have had the opportunity to know our bodies that we can bring in issues of control. Children need to discover all of the body parts that they possess and claim them as part of the self. To deny this discovery of genitals while allowing it for all other body parts will not promote growth and development. Later it will be fundamental in discovering sexual orientation by reflecting on the fantasies that start to occur during such self-pleasuring.

To start a process of control before a child has become capable of ownership and self-control is potentially damaging. For a child to have a conflict between a self-pleasuring drive and parental disapproval before adequate discovery of the drive may lead to what Freud called the repetition compulsion: the tendency to repeat some behavior often because its proper development did not occur in the first place. In a paradoxical way, prohibiting genital play too early can guarantee its excessive indulgence for many children later on. This is not to say that public genital play cannot be discouraged and modesty fostered, but the message needs to be: this is a private matter and should be done privately rather than not at all. An incorrect message can still do damage no matter how gently it is given.

Allen was a thirty-year-old architect who came to therapy complaining of a problem with masturbation and guilt feelings about it that he had experienced most of his life. He had been married for about five years, was happy in his marriage, and had one child. He claimed that he and his wife had intercourse once or sometimes twice a week, but it did not seem to be enough to satisfy him sexually. He said that in fact he would often be interested in sex again not long after having intercourse, but his wife was not interested.

His main concern was the strong guilt that he felt when he would masturbate, but in spite of this guilt, he could not control himself. His history went back to childhood. He recalled that his mother would retract his foreskin to wash him as he was uncircumcised. She would also scold him if he touched himself, which he quickly learned to do privately. One night when he was about nine, his father came into his room and caught him in the act of masturbation. His father became extremely upset, screamed that he would cut off his hands if he did it again, and prayed to God for his soul. This was extremely frightening to my patient, and for a while it had its prohibitive effect. But later on he resumed masturbation and turned to confession for forgiveness.

At first he would confess that he had disobeyed his parents because he did not know how else to refer to the masturbation. By about the sixth grade he learned such terms as self-abuse and impure touching to describe what he had done. The routine became quite regular, with self-abuse, guilt, and confession, followed by the same behaviors within a week or so, over and over again for years.

When he was about twelve years old he was masturbating almost daily and frequently would do it more than once. He could easily become stimulated again after an ejaculation and felt that he needed to relieve himself repeatedly until he felt "spent." He recalled one time when he was about fourteen actually masturbating twelve times, one after the other, and finally stopping because he felt that one dozen was enough. Part of the reason for his excess was to feel that if he were to completely satisfy himself he would be free from all sexual desire, which he knew rationally would not be the case. He also felt that as long as he had to confess, it was just as easy to say five as two, and maybe the extra few times would help him to go longer between confessions.

Finally he decided to stop going to confession and church regularly because it seemed so hypocritical. He sought psychiatric help because he thought there was no real value in confession while he still suffered considerable fear and guilt from the behavior.

This was a clear case of the repetition compulsion principle in operation due to the inappropriate interference by parents in a developmental process. The masturbation was compulsive because it was mixed with so many other emotions such as anger, fear, domination, and guilt. One of the strongest was an unconscious defiance, which was like saying to his parents, "You really cannot control me; I own my body and will use this way to prove it." Of course, the unfortunate part of the whole process was that consciously he did not feel he owned his own body at all, nor did he feel that he was in control. When this was finally worked out he would periodically masturbate, but he was not nearly so driven or guilt ridden. It also did not interfere as much in his life when he finally did acquire ownership and control. *God loves us unconditionally and simply wants us to love ourselves and each other.*

The fourth stage of development is called latency. The word refers to the notion that there is a repression of sexual interests at this time and a considerable sublimation of sexual energy into other activities — sports, social activities, and other creative endeavors. It occurs between the ages of six and twelve, allowing that some will go into puberty before twelve and some after that age. Authors differ on the extent to which sexual issues become unconscious at this time. Most seem to agree that some masturbation does persist, and that it is a healthy process for children to begin to deal with the conflict that develops as their superego or conscience informs them that their parents belong to each other and are not available for more intimate sexual activities with them. Some authors maintain that both the masturbatory activity and masturbatory fantasy are seen with great frequency in the normal child during latency, and almost universally from the age of eight on. Forcible suppression of masturbation with threats is usually regarded by analysts and psychiatrists as harmful.

If the oedipal conflict is resolved normally children will see that mother and father belong to each other and that they need to find their own partner in the world. If this particular conflict is not resolved internally, or, worse yet, if there is some actual sexual activity between parent and child, children will develop certain neurotic character traits as they grow older. These will interfere with their ability to form healthy sexual relations. Examples of such neurotic traits are: unconsciously seeking parental figures as persons to fall in love with, and then being continually disappointed; feeling that all intimate relations are unsafe and need to be avoided; and feeling guilty over appropriate sexual relationships and not understanding why.

If children give up masturbation and fantasizing without any internal work, such as seeing their body more realistically as they grow older, and do not give up parental figures as persons to fall in love with, they she may experience a reemergence of these issues later in life. If this does happen, the potential for continued development does still exist. However, it is often a period of confusion as they work on these psychological issues, and if they have made a commitment to marriage or celibacy prior to this re-emergence there may be additional problems to be resolved.

Theological integration

The Book of Ecclesiastes (3:1–8) says that there is a season for everything. I like to think of latency as the winter before the spring of adolescence. Many things are quietly sleeping before the warmth of spring hits and new life emerges. The latency child is preparing for the onset of adolescence by developing so many other parts of the mind and heart. There is a beautiful freedom and curiosity about many things during this time, and the mind, it is hoped, is developing the strength to deal with the turmoil of adolescence. It is a time for Cub Scouts and Campfire Girls, very special friends, and projects with parents. The joy of building a fort or treehouse and the kind of possessiveness that it brings is very important in learning separation, independence, and the creation of a world of one's own in fantasy as a preparation for the real thing. *God unconditionally loves us and simply wants us to love ourselves and each other.*

The fifth stage is adolescence. Here the teenager will pick up the issues of the repressed oedipal period with the added pressure of hormonal development. It is a time for dating and some experimentation with sexual relationships and intimacies. Masturbation is considered normal by psychologists for both adolescent boys and girls. It is a time when they can become fully appreciative of their sexual orientation, desires, stages of excitement, and orgasmic potential. It needs to be emphasized, though, that due to a variety of fears, adolescent psychosexual development can be delayed for many years.

Many of these adolescent issues are involved in what is referred to as the *masturbatory-fantasy complex*. For both males and females, masturbation, combined with the growing capacity of the mind to test reality, provides an opportunity for knowing, valuing, and accepting their maturing genitals. Here they can correct whatever misconceptions may have been created about their genitals during childhood. For example, a man may feel that his penis is too small to ever satisfy a woman, or a woman may fear genital damage from sexual intercourse because of her notion that her vagina is too small to accommodate the male organ. If these misconceptions persist, difficulties are likely to arise later in life when the person attempts a genital relationship.

Another important part of the masturbatory-fantasy complex is establishing genital predominance. Genital predominance applies to a developmental milestone that is equally important for males and females. The earlier analytic notions by Freud that suggested a dominance of male sexual development over females are no longer held. Genital predominance essentially refers to seeing all other forms of sexual activity, such as looking, touching, showing, kissing, smelling, sucking, and petting in the masturbatory fantasy as being preparatory to genital intercourse. These activities are generally referred to as foreplay, but in the fantasy they may assume a dominant position if there is fear of intercourse or if there is excessive pleasure associated with their performance. For example, a person may be able to achieve considerable sexual excitement from picturing a breast or a naked person, imagining prolonged kissing or touching or having oral sex, or being excited by some fetish, but be inhibited from imagining actual intercourse. Focusing on these foreplay activities rather than intercourse may be easier than dealing with whatever might be inhibiting the intercourse fantasy. This is applicable in some cases of homosexuality where members of the opposite sex need to be mentally avoided or seem unappealing for psychological reasons.

For the uninhibited intercourse fantasy to occur, these fears need to be worked through. The working-through may be a process that occurs both during and outside of masturbation. As part of the process there needs to be a clear development of sexual identity and orientation, a knowledge and familiarity with one's own anatomy and physiology, as well as an accurate appraisal of one's potential partner. The belief that sex is not dirty or shameful and a sufficient sense of ownership and control over one's own body are also helpful. When all of these issues are in place, we are able to give mutual consent and consciously and freely choose to participate in a range of sexual activities with an appropriate partner in appropriate circumstances, having first been able to rehearse them in our minds.

It might be useful to note that sometimes individuals are involved in masturbation without acknowledging it as such. A female obtaining genital pleasure by rubbing on a pillow between her legs or a male rubbing his penis against the mattress might not consider this as a form of masturbation. This can happen because of shame or ignorance. If masturbation is considered wrong, naming the activity might be avoided. It can be disturbing when such persons become conscious of what they are doing.

Given the importance placed today on relationships, it is necessary to emphasize that the masturbation-fantasy is part of a preparation for relationships. If the person one loves cannot be dealt with comfortably in one's imagination and the image of that person is distorted by repressed fantasies from the masturbatory-fantasy complex, then the relationship will become disturbed. This notion might be useful to those who assume a person is in a state of isolation and unrelatedness while masturbating. Granted, this can happen, but it is not the usual course of events. When it does happen, there are often other inhibitory personality factors involved that restrict one's imagination and capacity for relationships.

Theological integration

God created us physically capable of reproduction at the time of adolescence, and in some cultures it was not uncommon for adolescent marriages to take place. However, God also intended for couples to rear children and to have committed relationships, which suggests an intention for more development to take place than early adolescence has provided. It can be shown that some reach a maturity in later adolescence that will foster such responsibility and commitment for family and children. Today this is the exception, not the rule, in Western cultures. Especially with the demands for professional achievement, such early commitments are out of the question. It is usually tragic when adolescent impulses and desires get ahead of the potential for serious commitment and "babies start having babies."

God created adolescence as a time when the capacity for reproduction would be in place, but when the abilities to sustain a long-term committed love relationship and to rear and educate children are lacking. It is the time for establishing some of those abilities. It is a time for experimenting with relationships and for learning about closeness, physical contact, and consideration of others sexually. It is a time for establishing boundaries that are appropriate for an adolescent. It is a time for avoiding excessive inhibitions that will leave us with a sense of being deprived of a very special time as well as special relationships later in our lives. It is also a time when premature sexual indulgence will be damaging. Experiencing abandonment after a serious relationship can derail an adolescent's development. An unwanted pregnancy is always traumatic, whether it involves an abortion or the child has to be given up for adoption or is raised by the mother alone or even by both parents.

The venereal disease rate today among adolescents is a warning that many parents and adolescents are not acting responsibly. There was a recent documentary about teenagers in an affluent suburb. They ranged in age from twelve to sixteen, and they were engaging not only in a variety of sexual activities, but doing so in group settings. The whole matter came to light when one of the youngsters was diagnosed as having syphilis, and it was subsequently discovered that twenty of the group had become infected and needed treatment. Fortunately, syphilis is a treatable condition. If it had been AIDS the outcome would have been far worse. It was also revealed that the girls felt the boys did not have any regard for them and treated them in an abusive manner.

The question will certainly be asked here, "How can adolescents be helped to control themselves with all of the stimulation that comes not only from the hormones internally but from the environment?" The authoritative answer to that would be a best seller. But there are certain things that I think are essential even though some of them may not be popular.

Education. Education must always be age-appropriate and addressed to the issues that are of concern. If anything, parents and teachers underestimate what children and adolescents are concerned about and capable of understanding. This is being blatantly challenged, with intercourse being common in middle school youngsters. Children and adolescents need to know about sex and sexuality. There is a need for basic anatomy and physiology and psychology so that both sexes can understand each other. They will get the information one way or another, and sometimes it is by doing. Joan Timmerman wrote in *Human Development* magazine about a thirteen-year-old girl who learned what "blow job" meant by performing it on a fifteen-year-old boy. There is a mistaken notion that if children know about something they will then do it. It is more often the other way around. With the knowledge preceding activity there is at least some possibility for choice in the youngster's mind — and that brings up the second important issue.

Reasonable values. To tell adolescents that all sexual expression outside of marriage, including masturbation, is wrong and sinful is simply unrealistic. It will not be followed in today's society. It is important that they learn the value of love and commitment in a relationship before they become totally involved sexually. There needs to be established a healthy appreciation for the beauty of pregnancy for a couple that is willing and ready for a family. There needs to be respect for the dangers of unwanted pregnancies, AIDS, and the other sexually transmitted diseases.

Open communication is an important issue in controlling what goes on in all relationships, and it is certainly an important ingredient in what goes on in potential sexual relationships. Open communication as it relates to intimacy in more mature relationships will be discussed later, but for now it is important to consider that youngsters need to learn to talk about what is going on in their relationships and to be clear about what they might be doing sexually. Girls and boys should both learn the value of saying no to certain things when they themselves are not equipped to handle the degree of intimacy that is being approached. This will not only make for healthy adolescence, but will be an essential preparation for serious relationships later on. They need to learn how to communicate with each other about really important things, such as the necessity for commitment in sexual relationship. They need to know that it is important to learn a great deal about another person before starting a sexual relationship. They need to appreciate that having true love and caring for the other person is part of the psychological accompaniment for sexual intimacy. These are extremely important lessons that one would hope would be learned by adolescents to prepare them for a lifetime.

Theological integration

It is not helpful to place excessive emphasis upon sexual sins to assist in developing our sexuality. Adolescents may very well become frightened and guilty being told that consenting to enjoying sexual pleasure will send their souls directly to hell. It is very doubtful how much benefit it will have in controlling sexual activities, and it may very well have the liability of turning them away from faith and religious practices altogether. This is a common scenario. A major concern is that it takes away from the learning about interpersonal relatedness that is so essential to ultimately establishing sexual control and producing a mature person. *God unconditionally loves us and simply wants us to love ourselves and each other.*

The sixth stage is intimacy vs. isolation. There is a phrase from a beautiful hymn that goes, "You fill the hungry heart with gifts of finest wheat. . . . " This stage of development is about our hungry hearts, our longings, and our capacities for connectedness to others and God. In general there are two kinds of intimacies, physical and psychological. Both require that we have sufficient development so that our personal and physical identities are not threatened by the closeness involved. Boundary issues are very important here. We need to be able to let another in, and hold that person out, to whatever degree is appropriate for the relationship. We long for and yet fear this closeness, sometimes simultaneously. Céline Dion gets right to the heart of this issue in her song "Falling into You." As is suggested, the boundaries are gone. There is complete physical and psychological union.

Physical intimacy refers to the range of physical contacts that are possible and appropriate for humans again depending on the relationship. Warm hugging and affectionate touching of family members or friends are welcome and appropriate, whereas passionate kissing and genital touching are appropriate for lovers in the best sense of that word. There is a great deal of confusion in our present society about physical intimacy. I saw a television entertainment program in which a woman was brought to an emergency room unconscious and unidentified. A doctor recognized her as someone he had recently had intercourse with, but he did not even know her name. There had been no significant personal interaction, only sex. Unfortunately, this says something about our real society today.

Psychological intimacy is referred to by many authors as mutual self-disclosure. The word "mutual" needs to be emphasized here. Self-disclosure can occur unilaterally in some relationships, as it does with a psychiatrist and a patient or a priest and a penitent. This can often bring a feeling of closeness to one or both parties, but it is not intimacy. It occurs with someone that we feel comfortable being around and with whom we have things in common. There are feelings of trust and a mutual desire to see each other. Self-disclosure is gradual and more revealing as the friendship proceeds. It provides for a kind of stabilization as trials, tribulations, joys, and sorrows occur in our life. It helps us if someone is there to share them with.

Intimacy is the basis for love. A popular song several years ago expressed it quite well: "Getting to know you, getting to know all about you — Getting to like you, hoping that you like me." I think it is interesting and maybe more than coincidental that the Bible uses the word "know" to refer to sexual intercourse in the older translations: Adam "knew" Eve and she conceived (Gen. 4:1). Mary said to the angel, when she was asked to become the mother of Jesus, "How can this be, for I 'know' not man?" (Luke 1:34). When we start to fall in love we spend many hours in endless conversation. We share our life stories, our hopes and aspirations, our joys and sorrows, our pain and disappointments. Tremendous amounts of energy are expended. The other person is very much on our minds. As time goes on, and if a basic trust is there, we will even risk sharing a few secrets. The consistent response, but certainly not the only response, to this self-disclosure is understanding and acceptance. With understanding and acceptance comes a sense of well-being and a desire to reciprocate. A bond is formed.

For individuals, though, with some experience in attempting intimate relationships, some additional things might occur. As they "fall in love," they sense that this bond is growing. On the one hand there may be a fear of losing this special person. On the other there may be a fear of commitment and of limiting oneself to the other's growth and well-being. There is always a desire to see more of the other, to hear more of their life story, to know what is in their heart, and, when there is a sexual attraction, to see their body. The couple wishes that there be no barriers, psychological or physical, between them. They are approaching the point of wanting to 'know' each other in the biblical sense. Also, psychologically speaking, they will not be ready for that step unless there is a willingness for a commitment to the relationship. To give ourselves so completely to another and to have that person leave is one of the most painful experiences a human being can have. On the other hand, to share that love, and trust the commitment, is one of the most joyful and inspiring experiences we can have. And it truly needs to be that way. This is the "stuff" that families are made of.

Psychological intimacy without genital expression is certainly possible and is actually practiced by many celibates who are not suffering from developmental arrest or restricted growth. However, failure to develop the capacity for psychological intimacy will often lead to painful isolation and have unhealthy consequences. Some of these are expressed by Sandra Schneiders in her beautiful and thoughtful book, *New Wine-Skins:*

> Besides the immaturity that failure to engage the challenge to intimacy of adulthood involves, it also almost necessarily results in the displacement of intimacy needs in unhealthy ways. Over-dependence on and subservience toward superiors, reliance on authoritarian uses of power in work relationships, hypochondria, over-eating and addiction to drugs and alcohol, compulsive masturbation, drivenness in work, perfectionism.[14]

My wife and I have been married for forty-five years, and we are still getting to know each other because we are both still changing. I would describe one form of intimacy I experience with her as times when one of us is thinking and feeling out loud and the other is really listening. (This is definitely in contrast to the times when neither of us is open nor listening.) There is a sense of trust that anything can be said that we want to say. It will result at times in hilarious laughter, and at other times in unexpected tears, particularly as we recall some memories that have been painful. There can be flashes of anger or words of caution if some considered action seems dangerous or too outrageous. Sharing what we feel and think helps to clarify, which, although not always easy, is always helpful and healthy. What really matters to both of us is that we can communicate with each other in this way whenever we feel the need, and the other will be there. To me it is one of the most special aspects of being maturely in love. Over the years we have told each other many things, but we still keep learning as we grow older and things change. Some behavior patterns no longer exist. Some concerns of the past no longer matter, but new ones do. There will always be things to say to each other and I also believe that there are some things that we will never divulge. Keeping a few secrets is part of everyone's need for privacy and boundaries. These can be respected without an intimate relationship being compromised. As I was informed when I was a first-year psychiatric resident, being able to keep a few secrets is a sign of a healthy person. (The other signs were being able to eat and sleep, work and play, and make love.) Some things will be known only to God, and we may choose to be aware of God's intimate knowledge of us. We may also choose not to be so aware.

Theological integration

God created this potential in us so that we might experience the fullness of human relatedness. It is God's way of giving us an opportunity for connectedness so as to relieve some of the pain that we feel in being humans, always longing for another to share our lives with — lives filled with joys and sorrows, sickness and health, successes and failures. But most of all, intimacy helps us to satisfy some of the longing that we feel for the Spirit of God.

Charlie was a twenty-year-old college junior. He sought help with an uneasiness that seemed to have started with the beginning of his junior year. He really wasn't sure what it was all about, but he felt it might have something to do with his career or maybe his relationships with women. He had not declared any major in college until this year, when he decided on history because he felt it might be helpful in getting him into law school. He wasn't really sure he wanted to be a lawyer, but he felt the time had come for him to make up his mind about his future.

He also had an uneasy feeling about his dating patterns. He had managed to date a variety of girls since he entered college and readily admitted to having had a lot of sex that included petting, oral sex, mutual masturbation, and intercourse. He would usually date a girl until they had sex a few times, then he would begin to lose interest. He would simply stop calling, and if he ran into the girl he would just say that school was keeping him very busy. He and his friends had a great deal of fun talking about their conquests and sometimes would tell each other about certain girls who were "easy." He admitted some ambivalence about using condoms and had a slight concern about AIDS or getting someone pregnant, but really did not think that these were issues.

After several hours of therapy, it became clear that Charlie was terrified of psychological intimacy. He would manage superficial conversations long enough to be seductive and initiate the sexual relationship, but when the opportunity arose for him and a woman to get to know each other more as persons, he was terrified. He felt very inadequate as a person beneath his sexual bravado. He had little confidence in being able to get into law school and even less of making it through. His two years of avoidance had caught up with him. He had learned to use his sexual prowess to compensate for his feelings of inadequacy as a person.

It must be stated, though, that with the development of intimacy comes the potential for one of our most dreaded emotions: grieving over its loss. Dealing with the sense of loss goes back to infancy. Some people speak of the first loss as birth trauma, the sensations and pains that come right after birth. Be that as it may, there is no question that the process of losing the comfort of a constant and secure environment and being faced with many new stimuli can be painful as the baby's first cry, although joyful to us, indicates. There are many and varied opportunities for closeness in relationships as we grow. These may be brief or go on for some time. Sometimes we outgrow the need for the relationship. But to lose a meaningful relationship while it is very much alive is a painful experience. The more intense the bond that exists, the more pain that comes with its loss. To be human is to have *Necessary Losses*, as Judith Viorst so well describes in her beautiful and thoughtful book by that name.[15] *God unconditionally loves us and simply wants us to love ourselves and each other.*

The seventh stage is generativity vs. stagnation. As I thought about this stage I was reminded of two Latin axioms from college: *bonum est diffusivum sibi* (a good will share itself) and *nemo dat quod non habet* (we can't give what we haven't got). This is the stage of creating a new generation and all that goes into supporting it. From the intimacy of the previous stage comes the energy, desire, and commitment to continue the species. The love between two committed people will naturally tend toward their desire for a child. A popular song speaks to this when it declares that a women draws her life from a man and then gives it back again. Our capacity for this type of loving will depend on what our own family lives have been like. If we have not been loved very much it can be hard to love in later life. This is not to say that it is impossible, but we all carry a great deal of baggage from our past that clearly colors our present. Generativity applies equally well to those of us who are not involved directly in generating children but in creating the environment that allows them to thrive. Certainly, celibate priests, sisters, brothers, and other dedicated single people fall into this category. I must say parenthetically, though, that it is not the celibacy itself but love that provides this dedication. Celibacy creates a condition that allows love for others to be more easily expressed.

I think of Dickens's character Scrooge as a classic example of some-one fixated at the anal stage of development. I decided to present him here because he demonstrates how psychosexual development can become fixed and how that fixation effects later development. His miser-liness demonstrated his retentive self-centered character and his lack of love for anyone or any thing around him. Life was "bah humbug." After his conversion experiences, the scales fell from his eyes, and he could see true goodness and love and wanted to be a part of it. (We might say he jumped from stage two to stage seven overnight.) He had been totally wrapped up in himself and his wealth. His pockets were full, but his heart was empty. He denigrated the beliefs of others in order to avoid looking at the meaninglessness of his own life that was so lacking in re-lationships. When he recognized, after his terrifying dream, that he was not dead and still had a chance and the capacity to make a difference, his life changed profoundly. It could be said of any of us that once we see the real things in life, our generative capacities are called forth.

The most generative man I ever met is a Jesuit priest named Father Angelo D'Agostino, affectionately know to all as Dag. Dag was a sur-geon before he became a Jesuit, and during his regency he studied to become a psychiatrist. After he was ordained and I had returned from a stint in Vietnam, we both had private practices in Washington, D.C. Observing Dag at many functions, I always marveled at his energy. He had a full schedule of patients, and each evening he was involved with some committee meeting, seeing someone with a special need, or visiting with friends, but his purpose was unswervingly clear: the betterment of the others. After many years of practice in Washington, he started working with refugees in Thailand and then later in Nairobi, Kenya. It was in Africa that he ran across a situation that to him was completely intolerable: babies who were discovered to be HIV positive were discarded.

After getting no help from the African officials (who felt that because the babies were going to die, resources should not be spent on them), he established a little orphanage himself specifically to care for them. With some time and study a marvelous discovery was made. Over two-thirds of these children had the antibody to the AIDS virus, but they did not have the AIDS virus. Within a couple of years their systems would absorb the antibodies and they would become HIV negative. They were capable of leading normal lives. From the first few children, the orphanage expanded to its present number of eighty. Father Dag and his co-workers have established several cottages where the children can be raised with some semblance of family life. His orphanage is called Nyumbani, which means "Children of God." Of course, many who did in fact have the AIDS virus have died. There is a burial plot near the grounds of the orphanage. Seeing a television clip of the burial of a small child, with Dag presiding and the other children around, was one of the saddest and most inspiring things I have ever watched. His mission is truly to the poorest of the poor. These little ones had no home, no families, no possessions, and in many cases no health. His project has now become a model and will be established in Tanzania.

Recently Dag gave a talk to many AIDS workers from all over the world sponsored by the Franklin Graham Foundation. He described how the AIDS epidemic is wiping out the adult population in Africa, leaving many old people and children to fend for themselves. He proposed a "City of Hope," which would be a community of older people (perhaps acting like grandparents) living with the younger ones to create some semblance of family life. When he finished his talk Franklin Graham was so impressed that he immediately got up and expressed his interest in supporting the project with an initial donation of one million dollars.

Dag has spent some time living with us, and I found out the secret of his energy. It is his daily Mass. There he brings Christ into the world, and then he spends the rest of his day trying to do the same thing in his actions.

Theological integration

God created this generative potential in us for the sake of the next generation. It brings with it a very special satisfaction of giving back and a feeling that we are contributing to the well-being of those coming after us. It is a time when our experience and wisdom bear fruit that we hope will help leave the world a little better place than we found it. The energy for generativity often comes from an idealism that does not expect an immediate payoff as so many of the other stages do. In fact it may only be a hope that something of benefit will come after our life is over. *God unconditionally loves us and simply wants us to love ourselves and each other.*

The eighth stage is integration vs. despair. The main issue at this stage is that of watching life draw to a close. We need to be able to face death and the many losses it entails: of family, friends, possessions, positions, and finally of the body itself. If negotiated successfully we will see our lives as worthwhile and having some meaning. If not, despair may result.

When we speak of integration we are usually talking about what makes us whole. When a part is missing from anything, it is usually defective to some degree and may be defective to such an extent that it will not work. A car missing a door will still run, but a car missing a carburetor will not run at all. Very similar things can be said about the capacities that we need to function as human beings. Some parts are not very important, some are quite important, and some are absolutely essential.

Although we encounter this stage of integration as described above, the issue of integration, with its many different meanings, runs throughout our lives. It is often stated that if an issue pertaining to a particular stage, as in the case of Scrooge above, is not sufficiently integrated into our personalities as we pass through that stage, it will need to be integrated later, which generally speaking is a more difficult task. For example, if basic trust during the oral stage is not integrated, it will affect our ability to deal with the issue of control during the anal stage. If control during the anal stage is not integrated, it may well affect our ability to properly deal with gender issues occurring during the oedipal period. It is also easy to see that if basic trust is not established, everything following will be affected. It is like the house with a bad foundation. Everything above is jeopardized.

When we spoke about the masturbatory-fantasy complex of adolescence, we referred to a number of pregenital capacities that needed to be integrated into the fantasy in such a way as to establish genital predominance for the individual to be mature sexually. Integration is a big issue for those attempting to lead celibate lives, as will be discussed in detail later.

Integration can be discussed from a slightly more dynamic point of view by considering the concepts of fixation and regression. Fixation refers to our being stuck in a particular stage because there has been too much or too little pleasure and gratification in that stage so that we do not want to give it up and move on. Regression refers to our being so frightened or burdened by the issues of the next stage that we want to go back to a more comfortable place in our relationship and activities.

Theological integration

God gives many of us a long lifetime to get it all together and come to love ourselves, others, and, most of all, God. Getting the pieces of our lives in place using the talents, opportunities, and relationships given to us is what living is all about. We need some road maps to follow, which we can arrive at by reflecting on our development potentials and listening to the Creator through whatever faith is imparted in our lives. If we are open and attentive, the Spirit will not leave us wanting. *God unconditionally loves us and simply wants us to love ourselves and each other.*

Part II

Issues of Morality

Chapter 4

Sexuality and
Conscience Formation

To gain understanding of the basic issues of conscience we can do no better than to go to the *Catechism of the Catholic Church:*

> Deep within his conscience man discovers a law which he has not laid upon himself but which he must obey. Its voice, ever calling him to love and to do what is good and to avoid evil, sounds in his heart at the right moment.... For man has in his heart a law inscribed by God.... His conscience is man's most secret core and his sanctuary. There he is alone with God whose voice echoes in his depths.[16]

> Man has the right to act in conscience and in freedom so as personally to make moral decisions. He must not be forced to act contrary to his conscience. Nor must he be prevented from acting according to his conscience, especially in religious matters.[17]

> Conscience must be informed and moral judgment enlightened. A well-formed conscience is upright and truthful. It formulates its judgments according to reason, in conformity with the true good willed by the wisdom of the Creator. The education of conscience is indispensable for human beings who are subjected to negative influences and tempted by sin to prefer their judgment and to reject authoritative teachings.[18]

The long-standing Thomistic view of conscience is that we humans have the ultimate responsibility for deciding what is right or wrong for ourselves when it comes to moral actions. This view was reiterated by

Vatican II and teaches us to consider the teachings of the church, Tradition, Sacred Scripture, the sense of the faithful, reason, and natural sciences when attempting to decide upon the morality of particular actions. This is referred to as an informed conscience. From a psychological point of view this approach to conscience formation helps us to mature as human beings. It encourages us to have a broad view of reality, to be willing to investigate and tolerate divergent views, and finally to be able to draw moral conclusions that we are willing to be responsible for and to live with. Making up our minds in this way helps us to be respectful of various authorities while encouraging personal reasoning, freedom, and choice.

A rebellious adolescent cannot attain this broad perspective because the need to defy authority will overshadow all other issues. Likewise an immature dependent personality cannot do this because the need to please authority figures will predominate. Neither has established enough personal autonomy to live comfortably and assume the responsibility for his or her own conscience. We all need to be able to become parental figures for ourselves and give up the dependency of youth for our maturity to be completed. Or, as Freud put it when describing the maturing process, "Where the superego was, there ego will be." The mature individual takes over from the parent and other superego authority figures.

Individuals arrive often at difficult moral decisions with the assistance of pastoral guidance. These decisions are at times at variance with some official position whether that be Catholic, Protestant, Jewish, Hindu, Buddhist, or Moslem. My overall impression is that these discrepancies will always exist for one reason or another. St. Thomas observed many years ago that the further away we get from first principles in moral reasoning, such as "do good and avoid evil," the less certainty we encounter. These discrepancies will be fewer as the ways of preaching the Gospel or promulgating other religious or philosophical beliefs increasingly take cultural issues into consideration. As leaders listen more to the sense of the faithful (*sensus fidelium*) of all religious persuasions, and the Spirit speaking through them, the margins will lessen. These discrepancies will diminish as biblical and other scholars give us clearer understanding about what is false, misinterpreted, or pertinent to the affairs of a particular time, and as science contributes to our accumulated knowledge in a spirit of humility, discarding what is unsubstantiated in the light of new knowledge. God is one and truth is one. This is a long-standing philosophical and Catholic belief. But what is truth for one generation may not be so for the next, simply due to the blind spots in our intellects and our need to grow in wisdom.

It can sound so simple to say that we only need to review a few areas of thinking, make a judgment, and our conscience will have been formed. But to appreciate just how difficult the formation of conscience can be, we must study the workings of the mind, for it is in the various internal forces that the real difficulties in conscience formation can be found.

Because we are all human, these forces apply to those doing the teaching as well as those doing the learning and attempting to make a moral judgment. In other words, the experts need to be aware of how these forces might be affecting their teaching. Obviously if experts are refusing to look at material in another field, their credibility could be questioned as well as their authenticity. Room exists for honest differences of opinion in human knowledge, but it requires a conscious effort to see the other side and the whole picture.

Freud used two models of the mind at various times in his career. It is necessary to appreciate both of them and to study them separately in order to have a more complete picture of what happens to us mentally during conscience formation. His first model was called the topographical theory. He proposed that mental content could be either conscious, preconscious, or unconscious. Mental content is conscious when it is in awareness or can be brought into awareness with ease. It is preconscious when it can be brought into awareness with some difficulty. Such content often has a difficult feeling associated with it. Mental content is unconscious when it is completely out of awareness and no ordinary reflection can bring it into awareness. Such content would remain unconscious indefinitely, but might be brought to mind by some unusual event or circumstances, or be discovered through the process of free association, that is, saying everything that comes to mind, as is done in psychoanalysis. If an issue is not conscious it cannot be part of conscience formation.

Freud's later model was called the structural theory. In this model he defined three structures or areas of mental functioning: the id, the ego, and the superego. The id is the site of the aggressive and sexual drives referred to earlier: the sexual drives are the pleasure-seeking forces and the aggressive drives are the assertive forces that help us to get what we want and need in life. These often work in unison. The superego is a combination of our conscience, that which tells us right from wrong, and our ego ideal, the person that we would like to be in our minds. The ego is the mediator that looks for some compromise that will allow us to discharge our drives while taking into account the restrictions of the superego and the requirements of reality. The ego also invokes the various defense mechanisms that we use to control our anxiety.

Our conscience will often tell us that we may not have a certain pleasure or have it with a certain person. The id says, "I want it here and now." Then the ego comes in and says, "Not now with this person, but later with another." These basic structures are laid down in the mind by the age of six, but are continually modified throughout life.

With these ideas in mind we can now further appreciate some aspects of conscience formation. First of all, as stated earlier, we cannot make a conscious decision and assume moral responsibility without awareness. We do not sin in our sleep. We might have a notion about something nagging at us in the back of our minds, so to speak, and refuse to take it from preconscious to consciousness. In that case we might be responsible for the refusal. A businessman who sees an opportunity to make a large sum of money may not want to look very long, or at all, toward the people who could be hurt by such a deal. A theologian who has a tight moral theory might not want to look at the findings of science or the sense of the faithful while advocating the theory. Only when all the cards are on the table can we make informed moral choices.

The structural theory is also a conflict theory in the sense that we often find the superego and the id at war, with the ego mediating by bringing thought to the situation. However, during this process we often experience some type of anxiety or fear. It can be the fear of losing someone or something we love. It might be the fear of losing the love of someone important, frequently referred to as the fear of rejection. It might involve the fear of some kind of physical injury, or it might be apprehension over potential guilt feelings if we go ahead with what is contemplated. We can experience a kind of neurotic guilt, that is, guilt evoked by what we wish for rather than by what we plan to do or actually carry out. So we can see that having these models of the mind before us makes conscience formation a little more complicated.

Conscience formation is further complicated by our human nature. The Genesis story of Adam and Eve is seen as the fall by which humans developed a propensity toward evil. We do not need the Bible to substantiate this proclivity. We only need to look around and see that as humans we have strivings toward both good and evil, virtue and vice, growth and destruction present within us. We can respond to each other's needs in loving or hurtful ways in small or major matters. A spontaneous courtesy or a curt remark can color our days. We have selfless people, ethnic cleansings, and everything in between. One hopes that achieving more good than evil is our human goal.

Looking for and achieving what is good, however, is not always easy. St. Thomas, following Aristotle, said, *virtus stat in medio,* that is, virtue lies in the middle. We can sin by going to extremes. Freud spoke of the need for a certain amount of indulgence of our drives and a certain amount of deprivation if there is to be a healthy character development. We speak in psychiatry and medicine about a state of homeostasis where there is a kind of balance between various physical, chemical, and mental forces that gives us a sense of well-being. This sense of well-being implies we are in a good state of mental and physical health. Hence, when the ego is mediating properly between the id and the superego we enjoy a good state of mental health.

We can perhaps further illustrate this notion of balance by reviewing a concept that, while not in vogue too much these days, has merit when taken in the proper context. It is the notion of the seven capital sins. These seven sins are not sins per se but tendencies that could easily lead us into sin. These tendencies are pride, covetousness, lust, anger, gluttony, envy, and sloth. It is certainly true that these tendencies can lead to sin, but if we consider that it is really a balance of our tendencies as discussed above that produces virtue and well-being, it is possible to see that there is a potential benefit in these tendencies and that they do not necessarily lead to sin. This I will try to illustrate by going into detail.

Of course the capital sin of primary importance in our discussion of sexuality and conscience is lust. I chose to include some discussion of the others as well because of the fluidity of sexual energy. It can be shown that when there is an imbalance in one of these tendencies, it can also lead to an imbalance in another. As one concrete example, an excess of pride may cause a person to need many sexual conquests to feed this appetite. If one is slothful, she may not be willing to show the anger or aggression necessary for justice. If one is envious, it may lead to inappropriate seductiveness. If we are willing to thoroughly investigate our sexuality, we must be prepared to look in many different directions. Let us now examine each tendency in more detail.

Pride is a good thing. We take pride in our work, our families, and our friends. Children are the apples of their parents' eyes. Youngsters and adolescents take pride in their schools and defend them in athletic competitions. Pride becomes a problem only when it turns into arrogance and falls out of its balance. "Pride cometh before the fall." It is "my way or the highway." When we can't stand to have our egos bruised, we become averse to humility and truth.

Covetousness. The dictionary defines "covet" as to desire wrongfully. That is a very compact notion. Our earliest desires in life are to have something that belongs to someone else. If we say that is wrongful, we begin the guilting process too soon. We first need to be aware of all of our desires. Desires are not so much a matter of choice as they are periodic givens in our being. We need to recognize this. Desires arise from the id spontaneously and we need allowance to pick them up and deal with them before incurring judgment. In fact, I would go so far as to say that it is wrong not to be aware of our wrongful desires. We need breathing room in our souls for appreciating all of our wishes and desires. Once we have that in place, then we can be responsible for what we do with them.

When I was a youngster I had a cousin who bought a beautiful new convertible. When I saw it I felt an ache in my heart. I wanted it so badly. I don't believe that anyone would say that the desire was wrong. Most of us would probably agree that it was inevitable. For me the feeling was very painful, but very valuable. At that time I did not have enough money to buy a bicycle let alone a car. I was even too young to drive, but I certainly wanted to. What I did, in fact, have in front of me was a model of someone who had acquired a beautiful machine. It became a motivating force in my life, and I will readily confess that my first car, though far from new and expensive, was a convertible. I subsequently purchased several of them. If I had not been blessed in many other ways as well, I am sure the desire would have been strong enough for me to steal, if I had to, to get what I wanted. To add to the pain, not only did he have a beautiful car, but a beautiful wife, and an enviable profession as well. I was many years behind, but I had found a road map based upon desire.

Lust is an equally puzzling concept. The *Catechism* has this to say about lust: "Lust is disordered desire for or inordinate enjoyment of sexual pleasure. Sexual pleasure is morally disordered when sought for itself, isolated from its procreative and unitive purposes."[19] The importance that church places on this issue makes it necessary to understand as much about it as possible.

The dictionary defines lust as a sexual craving, especially excessive or unrestrained. Lust speaks to the overindulgence side of the sexual drive, but like the other tendencies being discussed the sexual desire can run the gamut. Humans are capable of becoming very sexually aroused or not aroused at all. There are sexual stimuli out there that can be very stirring to some individuals and hardly evoke a response in others. We need to distinguish between the sexual drive as a combination of ideas, impulses, and fantasies occurring within an individual, and their being implemented into sexual behavior. When we are lustful and experience an excess of sexual desire (which is not always easy to establish) there are usually other issues that are not being properly dealt with. If excessive sexual ideas and behaviors become chronic we can be considered sexual addicts or suffering from sexual obsessions (ideas, impulses, and fantasies) or sexual compulsions (when the ideas, impulses, and fantasies end in uncontrollable behaviors). Conversely, the sexual drive is equally pathological if an individual is so repressed from a conscious or unconscious fear of sexuality as to experience little or no sexual desire. (This would not be true of individuals who have made great efforts to consciously suppress their sexual drive and have been able to accomplish a high degree of control.)

It is useful to distinguish control in terms of suppressing desires and suppressing behaviors. Some individuals manage to suppress both. Others might control behaviors such as masturbation, but are still troubled by desires. There was a story circulated among us seminarians about the young priest who went to the eighty-year-old saintly confessor and asked him how long it would be before he would not be tempted against holy purity. The confessor replied, "My son, you will have to ask somebody older than me."

There are also individuals who by nature have a very low sexual drive. This would not be because of extreme repression, but a normal variant. I was once asked by a sixty-five-year-old priest if there was something wrong with him because he had never had sexual intercourse, had seldom masturbated, and felt very little difficulty in keeping his vow of celibacy. From our discussion there was nothing to suggest that he found sexual desires dangerous in any way. He simply had very few of them. Understanding that there is a variability of intensity of the sexual drive for most people we can now look to other issues and try to understand them.

One of the first things to consider is the object of the drive, the "who" or "what" that is sexually exciting. Usually the initial distinction here is whether the drive is toward individuals of the same sex or opposite sex, or both. In his book *Love Maps,* John Money speaks about our love objects, and the ways in which these love objects are laid down in our minds.[20] In each of our minds there is an image or images of an ideally sexually satisfying person, or sometimes it has to do with a sexually exciting thing, as in the case of a fetish. There are sexually exciting activities that we desire to perform with this person that need to be understood. Here we encounter the range of activities that are usually referred to as foreplay and intercourse. We looked at the precursors of these activities in our discussion of the masturbatory-fantasy complex. These images will produce feelings of desire, and many times the desire can be very intense. Trying to state whether such a desire is excessive or lustful, or appropriately intense and therefore very important in an individual's sexual life, can be difficult at times. Persons who are not acquainted with their sexual drive, objects of that drive, and the specific sexual activities they wish to perform are not in any position to channel, control, appropriately discharge, or suppress them. Intense sexual feelings construed as lustful by some might be considered a very important and healthy part of a sexual life by others.

When I was an intern I was called by a frantic nurse to see a patient who had just had a heart attack. The nurse claimed that she had walked into the patient's room and found the man's wife in bed with him. When

I approached the couple and asked about her need to be in bed with her husband, she said, "We have been married for eighteen years and have had intercourse every night for eighteen years. I am afraid that my husband will not be able to sleep without it." I reassured her that we would see to it that her husband would sleep, but for the moment his heart could not take the stress of sexual excitement.

The question of where individuals are in their sexual relationship will have a lot to do with the intensity of the sexual drive. The joke is sometimes made that if a young married couple put a nickel into a jar every time they had intercourse during their first year of marriage and took one out every time they had intercourse from the second year on, it would take a lifetime to empty the jar. (Obviously the couple above did not fall into that category.)

Our country has a divorce rate of 50 percent. Why is it so high? Of course, there are many factors, but one is that we often do not understand the natural fluctuations in our sexual drive. We need to identify what excites us sexually, and then find appropriate ways to incorporate it into our lives, that is, as long as it is not hurtful to ourselves or others and can be indulged without interfering with other aspects of our lives or violating values that we hold with our partners. This is another version of integration. If what excites us is hurtful or interferes, treatment may be necessary. If a man is sexually excited by a prostitute but not excited by his wife (the so-called Madonna complex), he is lacking in integration and the marriage is probably in trouble.

Doug was a forty-four-year-old writer who had been married about fifteen years and had two children. His marriage had been sexually declining for about five years. His wife was not interested in having sex, and he had recently become impotent with her, which caused him to question his masculinity. Their sex life had never been very satisfying, and it wasn't clear why. Now it was a huge problem. As many men do when they reach the so-called midlife crisis, he found a younger woman and started a relationship that in his case went deep into his soul. It started off rather gradually with meetings after work for a drink and conversation. He felt some guilt because of his marriage, but questioning where he was sexually seemed to be a greater need. Finally, they started a sexual relationship and his impotence disappeared. He could have intercourse with her three times in one afternoon. What he found was that she came closer to his masturbatory fantasy than any woman he had ever met. He hadn't even bothered to question what his wife was like sexually before they were married. He always denied that his wife's aversion to foreplay was a problem, but it was, and her infrequent need for intercourse led to his not feeling any need for her at all.

After he and his wife were divorced and he married his newfound love, passion continued intensely for about six months and then, as it usually does, died down. But there remained a certain kind of internal connectedness. There was a special kind of fit that made it possible for him to have an erotic and sexually satisfying relationship with her. Because he had prematurely labeled a healthy desire as wrongful lust, he failed to marry someone who could satisfy it.

Another perspective needs to be brought in here. That is the story of those who have formed a relationship with the person of their dreams and after a while become disillusioned as they see the real person and not the dream. John Hollis has written a book entitled *The Eden Project: In Search of the Magical Other,* in which he states that even when we are fortunate enough to find such a person, it will not always be paradise.[21] No matter how close others come to our ideals, they will still be individuals in the real world, with their own needs, aspirations, moods, struggles, and essential human frailties that can destroy the magic. Acquiring the ability to see through the ideal to real persons and to assist them with their own struggles, sometimes at the expense of our own gratification, is to love in the purest sense of the word and makes for a maturing and enduring relationship.

In my opinion there is an inherent problem in the church's view of lust. It proposes that sexual desire is morally disordered when separated from its procreative and unitive purposes. That statement presupposes a high level of sexual maturity. The question arises as to how that maturity can be achieved if the first legitimate experience of sex is after one is married. Everything that was stated above — about knowing the objects of desire in an emotional and not just intellectual way, knowing something about the types of fantasized activities that would satisfy that desire, and being familiar with the intensity of that desire is regarded as sinful. It demands a continual repression or suppression of the sexual drive until marriage in order to avoid sin. Then it presupposes that the drive will be mature and ready for procreative and unitive purposes.

There is no room to enjoy sexual pleasure, even for educational purposes. Our experiences have taught us otherwise. I do not believe that we are capable of committing an intimate part of ourselves to another without knowledge, familiarity, and control of that part. To know thyself must apply to our sexuality also.

Anger. When Christ entered the temple and drove out the money changers, saying, "You have made my Father's house a den of thieves," he gave us a beautiful model for anger. Christ was not afraid of his anger, demonstrating it as a good and healthy emotion. Anger is one of the safeguards of life in the relational world. A mother cub will fight for her young. A man will vigorously defend his family and property. We often do have to fight in various ways to keep ourselves alive. Sometimes it is as simple as kicking ourselves out of bed in the morning to go to work. At other times it may be as difficult as attacking a drug problem that is destroying ourselves or someone we love. There is some truth in the concept of "survival of the fittest," and being the fittest includes having a facility with healthy aggression.

One of the interesting things about anger is that it can be directed outward toward others, as in protecting our life or property, or inward toward ourselves, as in the kick to get to work or start studying. It can take the form of guilt when we feel we have used anger inappropriately toward others or make us feel depressed if a self-directed anger is on-going. It can be directed at others, for all the fear-based reasons stated above in the structural theory, when we are mobilizing ourselves to protect what we psychologically value. Many times we don't even recognize the fear and we go directly to the anger. We are equally capable of fight or flight. Our education and experience may lead us to one more readily than the other. Nevertheless, when we fight we often feel like fleeing, or when we flee we often feel like fighting. When anger turns to rage it can be a destructive force which is capable of going beyond what is required for survival. When anger turns to self-hatred it can destroy a person through depression and the value of self-criticism is lost. The necessary moderation in anger is easy enough to see, but often hard to achieve.

Repressed anger is a very common and difficult problem in psychology, and there is considerable material available about it for anyone interested. There are some cases where the lack of appropriate anger is exasperating. I do not believe that even Christ would encourage a woman who is being abused by her husband to turn the other cheek. He would wonder why she loved herself so little as to put up with such abuse. It is always healthy to be able to feel our anger, as with all other feelings. When we can feel it, we can decide what to do with it. One hopes it will mostly be used for the protective purposes for which it was intended.

Anger is an impulse that can be quite intense and immediate, and it needs to be guided by reason. I can best illustrate this by a personal example. A friend and I were walking home from a night football game. As we approached our car, two men stepped out from the darkness and asked for our billfolds. I said I did not want to give up my billfold and kept on walking. One of them instantly started to remove a pair of binoculars from my friend's shoulder and knocked him to the ground. To put it simply, I saw red. I went on the attack, throwing myself into him in an attempt to get him away from my friend. We started exchanging blows and after a few moments both men fled.

Upon reflection I realized this was a very impulsive and stupid act. I could have gotten both of us shot or killed if they had a gun. As it was, I ended up with a black eye, my friend got a bruised arm, and my glasses were so badly damaged that it cost me a couple of hundred dollars to replace them. I have thought a lot about this incident, and one thing is clear. The sight of my very good friend down on the ground with this person attacking him was intolerable. The bond of friendship was very strong and went back several years. Unfortunately, I did not reflect upon the potential consequences of my attack. But why was I so defiant with them in the first place? Why was I reluctant to attempt some negotiation in the beginning such as, "Here is the money, but let us have our billfolds." I hate to say it, but I regarded them as thugs who were beneath me, and I did not want to have anything to do with them. So not very far from the anger is arrogance. Less arrogance and more charity would have been much more helpful here.

Gluttony is a very basic tendency. In this day and age we see it in the form of bulimia, binging on food; in days of old, during the Roman Empire, they had their vomitorium for purging after feasting so they could feast again immediately. The other extreme of gluttony, of course, is anorexia. Persons with this condition will literally starve themselves, at times to death, because they have the notion that they are fat and ugly even as they are carrying around bodies that are emaciated.

The oral drive is the first to appear, and life itself depends upon it. I never appreciated the concept of breast envy until I started giving bottles to my granddaughters. They would grab their bottle with their tiny little hands the way they had grabbed the breast, and then close their eyes sucking with great vigor and cooing in what could only be contentment as they were satiated. It is not hard to see how eating and being loved go together. And this continues through our lives. We have family meals and dinner parties with friends. The body and soul get nourished together. So the question arises, why gluttony? We need too much of a good thing when something else is missing in our lives, and that something very often is love. In working with bulimic patients it wasn't hard to trace how the impulse to eat was tied to parental struggles. Feeling undervalued or criticized is one way it can get started. If the condition becomes known to the family, it may also be a source of derision. One father would frequently ask his bulimic daughter if she had been doing any of that "secret eating."

Of course the oral drive can be overindulged with alcohol as well. In the film *Leaving Las Vegas*, Nicholas Cage took a shopping cart and went tearing through a liquor store filling the cart. He immediately rushed home and started drinking as though he were parched. This would continue until he felt some internal quiet, and he would fall asleep only to begin again when the tiger awakened. Many addictions with alcohol or drugs end in suicide, either accidental or deliberate. Sometimes it is both alcohol and drugs.

I tend to think of gluttony as a consumer problem. The oral drive, as any other, can be overindulged or it can be displaced or diverted to many valuable and beautiful things in our life, including God. We may wish to consume to excess when our hunger is intense and when we are not feeling satisfied, but we may be needing something else besides food. For example, we may have undischarged anger or lust. We may feel empty from a lack of self-esteem. We will all experience hunger and dissatisfaction at times in our lives, but we need to continually seek to be filled so as to keep physically and spiritually nourished without becoming a glutton for anything — including punishment. (It is sometimes useful to remember that even punishment can be preferable to isolation in a relationship.) The continual discernment of what we truly need is a challenge for all of us.

Envy is so akin to covetousness that they really could be considered together. Envy is defined as the desire for another's advantages or possessions. These two ideas imply another notion, and that is jealousy. Jealousy is the desire to have a relationship with a person who is attached to someone else. A distinction between jealousy and envy that is sometimes made is that jealousy refers to relationships while envy refers to things. All three: covetousness, envy, and jealousy, refer to our possessiveness. Going back to the structural theory, our first impulse, coming from the id, is to take what we desire. This is countered by the superego saying, "No. This is not yours." The ego then comes in and tries to mediate by saying, "Let us see how we can get some form of this for you and what it will take to do so." The ego attempts to tell us how to handle these feelings.

We are all familiar with cases of the spouse who is jealous over a neighbor's relationship with his or her own spouse, and the moves that are begun to try to attract the desired party. This usually ends in disaster and the destruction of one or both families or sets of friends. This feeling can lead us either to improve our present relationship, if we are committed to it and want to work on it, or to seek one that is similar to what is envied, if we are free to form a relationship. One thing that I think is essential for establishing a good and healthy relationship is the freedom to do so. That means no conflicting interests if one is married, committed, or engaged. If we are in a relationship that is not working, it is essential to either make it work or get out *before* beginning another. People today are searching, finding, loving, discarding, and then repeating the patterns. They haven't taken time to examine basic envy, jealousy, and other unresolved emotions, so that they might know what they want and get into a relationship that can offer some hope of achieving their wants. Once in such a potentially good relationship, it will still take effort and commitment to make it work.

Sloth is defined as extreme or habitual indolence, or a disposition to avoid exertion. I tend to think of it as a form of interference with our naturally assertive tendencies, or interference with the aggressive drive. When we are sexually (in the broadest meaning of that term, that is, seeking pleasure) and aggressively free we tend to work and play without interference. When we are afraid of those drives and the proper sublimation of those energies is interfered with, then we become inhibited people. All of us have had the experience of not wanting to get going on Monday morning because the weekend has not been very restful or we have partied too much. But with a little push we can get ourselves running. When a person is in a state of habitual "Monday morningness," something is wrong. It could be a number of things, such as depression, fear of really engaging in work, preoccupation with some other problem, or a medical condition. Fortunately, for this tendency as well as many of the others that are manifestations of psychiatric problems, there are medications that can help to overcome the difficulty, often combined with psychotherapy.

Work in itself should not be a problem and as a matter of fact can be very satisfying. It gives our life focus and purpose. Satisfying work, with all other things being equal, can even be energizing. When I was practicing psychiatry and psychoanalysis, there were times when I felt at the end of the day that I could begin it all over again without any trouble. Everything had gone well and I was able to keep a certain equilibrium. There were other days when all had not gone so well. The energy was gone, and I needed to get refueled.

Of course, there is the motivation and consequent energy that comes from the need to make money to support ourselves and those who depend on us. Unfortunately, at times, even the need to make money will not push us through real inhibitions to work, any more than the alcoholic can stop drinking because his family isn't getting enough money for food.

Like all of the other tendencies, sloth has an opposite extreme in what we have come to call workaholism. Driven by greed, the need to flee from personal problems or relationships, the fear of being alone, or a pleasurable rush of adrenaline, we can throw ourselves into our work and spend many hours paying little attention to other things. A busy doctor or executive can easily justify his absence from his family by the demands of the job. But often that personal need to be so committed to work will carry a price tag: the loss of valuable things in our lives such as important relationships with family, friends, and even ourselves.

When my children were trying to decide what fields to enter in college, I gave them only one piece of advice. I suggested that they go into something that they were interested in. If something holds our interest, there is a good chance that we have a talent for it. We usually do not stay long with things that bore us or that we feel inadequate pursuing. If we have the interest and the talent, we will usually be successful because we will stick with that endeavor until it yields the desired results. And finally, if we have interest, talent, and success in production, money will be made. But the essential thing is the interest. Given the fact that we spend anywhere from one-third to one-half of our lives in work, and sometimes even more, it pays to pursue what will provide interest and satisfaction. We hear stories all the time about those of us who, for whatever reasons, have not been able to achieve that combination. Individuals may appear as slothful, but it may be something much deeper.

Richard Sipe addresses the role of work in the lives of celibates, but his observation can be useful for all of us:

> Work is the natural basis of the spiritual life. One primary command delivered to Adam was to work — to labor. Some have mistakenly interpreted this divine directive merely as a punishment for sin. It is far more than that. A person's celibacy is inextricably bound up with work, with the fact of work as mastery — the productive use of one's energies and time — rather than with any particular task. Work forms a program for survival and salvation. It is part of the program for living and giving life to others. Work channels our natural talents and our resources, interests, and experiences into useful and productive means of interaction with others.
>
> David was a shepherd, Jesus a carpenter — most of the apostles were fishermen. Paul was proudly a tent maker. Their preaching and teaching did not denigrate or even obviate their other work. Preaching, studying, and writing were extensions of their ability to achieve mastery, live, and promote life. There is something dehumanizing in the loss of respect for work. Lack of respect for work undermines any spiritual life because it diminishes respect for self and others in an essential area of existence and mutual interdependence.[22]

The issue of sloth and workaholism can make for some interesting appearances in those leading celibate lives. Given freedom with their impulses, celibates will pursue the tasks of their vocation with a certain vigor. However, it is quite possible for a priest to hole up in his rectory with little more responsibility than a daily Mass, if that, because he can be supported by the system. A brother or priest in a monastery can spend considerable time alone in his room, in front of a television or computer, with little productive work being accomplished. Others may know about these patterns and either fail to confront them or find that it does no good. I point this out with the greatest of compassion for the priests who are suffering from some serious psychopathology and in need of treatment. Unfortunately, some are so rigid in their ways that they do not even see the need for help, a phenomenon that is not confined to celibates or single people.

At the other extreme are those who hardly ever stop. They go from one task to another, often squeezing in things for which there is really no room, sleep a few hours, and start the whole routine all over again. The essential feature of the workaholic is avoidance. Amid all their work, workaholics are starving spiritually and greatly in need of finding God and being renewed by the Spirit, who has been lost somewhere in the paperwork files.

IT IS NOT ALWAYS EASY for us to see the extremes of the seven capital sins in our minds and hearts, but if we are honest they can be recognized. We don't like to see these attitudes in ourselves because they can make us feel guilty or immature. We are also quite capable of rationalizing to throw a more favorable light on their existence. When attitudes or tendencies are present without our deliberate choice we really cannot call them sins, but having the courage to recognize them will help us to avoid their coming into our actual behaviors. If we focus only on our basic loving tendencies, we can easily be thrown off track.

I offer the following examples as illustrations of these seven unflattering tendencies of our nature, and I am reminded of what St. Paul said when considering them: "For I know that good does not dwell in me, that is, in my flesh. The willingness is ready at hand, but doing the good is not. For I do not do the good I want, but I do the evil I do not want" (Rom. 7:18–20). Again, keep in mind that the attitudes can become a problem by moving toward either extreme.

Pride. I am better than you because I am white and you are black. I am a Christian and you are a Moslem. I am a man and you are a woman. I am a Westerner and you are Asian. I am smart and you are dumb. I am a professional and you are a laborer. The basic flaw in all of these unloving attitudes is pride and prejudice. Reverse side: You are better than me because you are white and I am black. You are a man and I am a woman. You are a Westerner and I am an Asian. You are smart and I am dumb. You are a professional and I am a laborer. Again the basic flaw is prejudice and a false humility. The helpful attitude is not to confuse difference with goodness or badness, superiority or inferiority. All of our human qualities, good characteristics, and talents are from God. All of our gifts are needed and one is no better than the other. A gardener might be holier in God's eyes than the learned president of a university where he tends the grounds. They need each other.

Covetousness. I want what you have right now and I do not want to work for it. Reverse side: There is no sense in wanting. I never achieve anything anyway.

Lust. I will use you sexually and not provide any love in return. Reverse side: I will not expect sexual relations from you even though we are married.

Anger. I will hurt you because you are in my way and I am the only one who matters. Reverse side: I cannot feel anger no matter what happens.

Gluttony. My pleasure is all that matters. If it hurts my health or others starve, I don't care. Reverse side. I can't stand the way I look, so I will not eat.

Envy. You have what I want and I hate you for it; I will take it from you, or, make you suffer because that is what you are doing to me. Reverse side: I don't care what I have. I will only lose it in the end anyway, so what difference does it make?

Sloth. I expect to be given what I want. I am special and should not have to work. Exertion is beneath me, but my needs have to be answered. Reverse side. I have to keep busy all the time because I have to always be accomplishing something to feel worthwhile.

Richard Sipe quotes from John Milton's "After the Fall":

One who can apprehend and consider vice with all of its seeming pleasures, and yet abstain, and yet distinguish, and yet prefer that which is truly better, is the true wayfaring Christian.[23]

I consider those lines as a very poetic expression of integration in the middle road.

Chapter 5

Sexuality and Masturbation

Masturbation has been a subject of interest for centuries. It has been shrouded in false information and condemned by medicine, the church, and society, yet persistently practiced with guilt, shame, and trepidation. More recently, because of the pejorative connotations which the word "masturbation" carries, "self-pleasuring" has been substituted. At the turn of the twentieth century it was believed that about three-fourths of the diseases known to medicine were caused by masturbation. Freud was one of those believers. By the end of his life he had changed his mind, largely because the analytic method, which he discovered, shed light on something that had never before been studied: the masturbatory fantasy. He saw the mental processes in masturbatory fantasies comparable to the mental processes in dream formation. Freud viewed the analysis of dreams as "the royal road to the unconscious." Similarly he discovered that analyzing masturbatory fantasies could reveal a great deal about a person's wishes, sexual orientation, and some personality traits.

It would seem that the positions of many church leaders and the psychological community are at opposite poles when it comes to masturbation. The Catholic Church's official teaching regards masturbation as an intrinsically disordered action that can never be objectively justified; psychology regards it as action that is normal and at least helpful, and some feel even necessary, for psychosexual development.

The *Catechism of the Catholic Church* says this about masturbation.

By masturbation is to be understood the deliberate stimulation of the genital organs in order to derive sexual pleasure. "Both the Magisterium of the Church, in the course of a constant tradition, and the moral sense of the faithful have been in no doubt and have firmly held that masturbation is an intrinsically and gravely disordered action. The deliberate use of the sexual faculty, for whatever reason, outside of marriage is essentially contrary to its purpose." For here sexual pleasure is sought outside of "the sexual relationship which is demanded by the moral order and in which total meaning of mutual self-giving and human procreation in the context of true love is achieved" (CDF, *Persona humana,* 9).[24]

This is clearly a statement based on an action-centered morality, for although the term "relationship" is used, there is no attempt to refer to the many factors that go into a loving relationship and the many considerations that govern rational procreation. However, later in that same paragraph the *Catechism* goes on to state:

> To form an equitable judgment about the subject's moral respon-
> sibility and to guide pastoral action, one must take into account
> the affective immaturity, force of acquired habit, conditions of
> anxiety, or other psychological or social factors that lessen or even
> extenuate moral culpability."[25] This is clearly a statement based on
> person-centered morality.

Some theologians have contradicted this teaching in various ways: Father Charles Curran has investigated and challenged the notion that masturbation is an intrinsically grave sin. He concludes that masturbation is not always a grave matter, an action which is *ex toto genere suo grave.*[26]

Norbert C. Brockman, S.M., summarizes several nuances:

> Masturbation is far from being a simple sexual sin, but is part of
> the complex process of maturation. While it is always objectively
> sinful, habitual masturbation usually involves a significant dimin-
> ishing of freedom, so that in many cases it is unwise to consider
> the person who has this problem as being morally responsible, at
> least in regard to serious sin.
>
> While masturbation is a moral question, for the average person
> it is not necessarily to be regarded as seriously sinful. A partic-
> ular individual action has meaning insofar as it makes incarnate
> and intensifies the fundamental moral choice that man must make

between God and creatures, which ultimately means self. It is difficult to imagine that an act of masturbation could be regarded as such a fundamental choice.[27]

Adolescence is a time for confronting one's sexuality. For this to happen, adolescents must develop values that will govern their sexual behaviors and experience appropriate guilt feelings when these values are violated. However, guilt feelings are part of the masturbatory-fantasy complex. There are factors, conscious and unconscious, rational and irrational, influencing their formation, and the adolescent may need help in sorting them out.

If an adolescent is taught that masturbation is wrong and is intrinsically evil, that is, not justified under any conditions, there indeed will be guilt feelings. These guilt feelings may prevent some important psychological processes from being dealt with, such as reflection on sexual orientation and learning about the images that bring sexual excitement as a type of preparation for a real relationship. If there are inappropriate fantasies, such as ones dealing with children, or beating fantasies, the adolescent might be more willing to seek some help if the whole process was not regarded as evil to begin with. The work of adolescence requires that we find an appropriate sexual object in real life, and masturbation is a kind of prelude to that search. As stated under the adolescent stage of development, this act is often not an isolative thing (because of the mental activity accompanying it) but more a preparation for the foreplay and intercourse of later life. This is by no means to suggest that there cannot be serious problems with masturbation in adolescence, but these need to be addressed as clinical issues.

Most adolescents masturbate in spite of whatever admonitions they give themselves against doing it. It speaks to the strength of our natural tendencies for development. The process can be helped rather than hindered by appropriate teaching and guidance. If an adolescent does feel that it is sinful to masturbate, he or she may have a need to confess. If the confessor or teacher reinforces the official teaching about masturbation without the pastoral counsel that is suggested, it will teach the adolescent a lot about guilt, but little about sexuality. When adolescents do feel guilt, they may benefit from the theological opinion that not every act of masturbation is a mortal sin or, better still, the theological positions such as the "neutral attitude" articulated by Brockman: "Masturbation is such a normal part of growing up that the only serious evil that can be attached to it arises from the unfortunate guilt feelings that come from early training and negative attitudes toward sexuality. Masturbation represents a phase through which a person grows toward interpersonal relationships."[28]

These remarks may help an adolescent to focus on other issues besides guilt and to continue the work of the psychosexual development and integration discussed earlier. It may indeed be easier for the adolescent to focus on guilt than to face the challenge of further maturation, particularly if there is some psychological conflict around sexual orientation or the particular fantasies that the adolescent finds stimulating. Again it may be helpful to note that adolescent sexual development does not necessarily occur during adolescence, and this same approach may be helpful to adults who are struggling with adolescent issues.

As has been pointed out earlier, sexuality is God's way of calling us into communication with each other through love and procreation. Thus we must guard against self-centeredness and self-preoccupation. There are times, though, when masturbation will not interfere with any of these ends and may in fact enhance them. Studies show that intercourse is more frequent with couples who also masturbate, thus dispelling the false idea that masturbation is necessarily isolative and interferes with intercourse. It can be a harmless act, or even an act of self-love, done solely for pleasure, or to confirm one's sense of sexual identity, or to release sexual tension that has become intolerable. (The tension may in fact be distracting from important interpersonal issues or work-related matters.) It may be done to help one sleep and be more rested for the next day. Guilt feelings and the fear that one has lost the "state of grace" by masturbating can be very self-punishing and may likewise interfere with sleep. As I have listened to so many people struggle with this kind of guilt I have often thought that we would be so much better off, have much more peace of mind, and be healthier in our development if we were taught to make an act of thanksgiving for the gift of our sexuality instead of an act of contrition after masturbating. We could be grateful to God for our marvelous organs and the pleasure they give us. Adolescents should pray for someone with whom they can share this pleasure as they mature and seek to discover the person of their dreams in a future mate.

There are times when acts of masturbation might be used to relieve sexual tension that might otherwise be released in inappropriate or even harmful ways. A young man very sexually aroused by a woman he is trying to court and establish a healthy relationship with might choose to masturbate rather than press her for intercourse that he sees as premature and possibly resulting in a pregnancy which neither of them could support. A married man away from his wife might be tempted to have a liaison with an available woman or engage a prostitute to relieve his sexual tensions. He chooses to masturbate as a safeguard against infidelity and the possibility of contracting AIDS or other sexually transmitted diseases. Contraction of some of these diseases puts us at risk of spreading them to any sexual partner in the future.

None of these acts of masturbation would interfere with the main purposes of sexuality in marriage unless it is insisted that each and every act of sexual expression needs to be open to procreation and expressing love to another. Such insistence would seem to be a shift back to an action-centered morality and away from a person-centered morality, or away from the order of reason and back to the order of nature. Masturbation in such cases may indeed have nothing to do with loving and committed relationships, and these individuals may be generative in many aspects of their lives. Some who masturbate may even have commitments to celibacy and their lives are thus filled with generative activities, but occasionally the need for some sexual release is overwhelming.

Another dilemma might arise when one considers the acts of mutual masturbation between married couples. Masturbation here may indeed be a very loving action that may not lead to intercourse. An ejaculation outside of the vagina could be interpreted as a form of contraception because the action does not allow for procreation. At the same time it fulfills the other purpose of sexual expression in marriage called "mutual support."

I am sure that there are those who will object that evil may never be done that good might come from it. Therefore they can never entertain the proposition that some good can come from masturbation. This position is an abuse of a principle wherein the labeling of evil is imposed and then serious consequences follow from it — with the proponents of such a position shrugging off any responsibility. The principle may be sound, but I am suggesting here that evil is not automatically established by the object or purpose of an action. It needs to be further considered in terms of the circumstances and consequences and intention of the person performing the action. The principle can actually be harmful when evil is determined based on the concept of intrinsic evil. For example, the denial of sperm testing to a couple attempting to conceive a child because it involves masturbation would ignore crucial interpersonal issues for the sake of an abstract principle. These couples are in fact trying to achieve the procreative purpose of marriage.

My overall impression is that masturbation is part of the human condition, as Francis and Marcus so well express by the title of their book, *Masturbation from Infancy to Senescence.*[29] It enhances our development for sexual relationships. It provides some occasions for pleasure that do not interfere with the major purposes of sexuality. If it is primarily treated as a sinful issue, it can become a subject of major moral and psychological conflict, not infrequently causing harm in one's life. If our main attention is given to our abilities to work, play, and most importantly to love, with masturbation acquiring significance only insofar as it interferes with these greater goods, we would be healthier, happier, and holier people.

Chapter 6

Sexuality and Homosexuality

Frank was a twenty-one-year-old, white male who for several years was greatly distressed because he felt sexually attracted to males instead of females. In spite of efforts to develop a heterosexual attraction, his homosexual interests persisted. Although he never acted on any of his impulses or fantasies, he carried around painful feelings of guilt and shame. These feelings were constantly reinforced by family members who disparaged homosexuals and by other males who themselves were very macho and proud of their attraction to women. He never felt safe to confide his pain to anyone inside or outside his family but simply carried the burden by himself. As his hopelessness increased about ever being able to change his homosexual orientation or live a celibate life comfortably, he became suicidal and finally killed himself, leaving a note to explain his unresolvable conflicts.

Gene was a thirty-year-old white male who sought therapy for depression and periodic homosexual episodes with males other than his forty-five-year-old partner of the last five years. His homosexual orientation went back as far as he could remember. He preferred playing with dolls rather than trucks or bicycles. He was comfortable only in the presence of his mother, and he always suffered from the criticism of his father, who called him a "sissy." Anyone looking at him would be inclined to make the judgment that he was homosexual. He was aware of this, but not ashamed of it. He felt strongly that he was what he was, but his emotional problems centered on the conflicts in his committed relationship that were very similar to those of a heterosexual relationship. His partner was not nearly as interested in sex as he was and would often refuse him, which clearly would be a factor in his seeking other men for sexual activity. His guilt was quite strong, but anticipating it was not a sufficient deterrent against sexual encounters. He had neither the interest in nor any hope of changing his sexual preference for men, but he made it clear that he needed psychiatric help for depression and anxiety. With medication and psychotherapy these symptoms did improve as did his sexual adjustment.

Harold was a twenty-six-year-old Jesuit scholastic who was having his teaching experience between philosophy and theology as Jesuits do. He presented himself to me as a homosexual who thought he had better leave his order because he was becoming more attracted to men as he grew older; now that he was in a setting of high school boys, this homosexual orientation seemed to be intensified. He stated that he didn't date much in high school and was never really bothered by sexual thoughts, nor did he have any sexual experiences other than occasional masturbation. He was somewhat vague about the nature of his masturbatory fantasies but allowed that at times he might think about women. I suggested that he delay any decision about his vocation and enter into psychotherapy twice a week. Two years into his therapy he said he felt again the need to leave his order, but this time it was because he had fallen in love with a woman and hoped to get married.

Father John was a forty-five-year-old priest who had been in his community for about twenty years. He came into therapy wondering whether he should remain a priest. He was much younger than other members of his community and was convinced that he was homosexual. He was also feeling a great deal of anger toward the church because of its attitude toward homosexuals. He felt that he was definitely called to the priesthood, but his frustrations with his community and the rigidity of some members greatly disturbed him. He had trouble finding friends among his fellow priests but was comfortable with homosexuals and heterosexuals who could accept his homosexuality. He visited homosexual bars on occasion with these friends. Although he did not habitually have homosexual relations, he did on some occasions.

It was interesting to note during therapy that he was unaware of any sexual feelings until he was in his late teens. He then started to masturbate and had heterosexual fantasies during the masturbation. He made a few attempts to date girls but was unsuccessful because of his awkwardness. When he was about twenty-five he found that men were attracted to him. This was flattering and gratifying compared to the rejection he felt from women. The whole question of his sexual orientation was really left unanswered when he decided to become a priest. He figured it would not matter because he would be celibate. However, it did matter, because he found that some men in his community were attracted to him, and this led to intermittent homosexual encounters. Now that he was considering leaving the priesthood, the question of whether he was a homosexual or a heterosexual was revived. His conclusion after considerable therapy was that he was actually bisexual.

Many authors point out that it is probably more accurate to speak of homosexualities rather than homosexuality. This is not a new idea, but it seems to be a difficult one for us to understand. There seems to be some psychological need to make the term singular instead of plural. There has been media coverage of what is called "conversion therapy," namely, a therapy that claims to be able to convert a person's sexual orientation from homosexual to heterosexual. In one television program two people were submitting opposite results from their therapy. One was stating that his orientation had been changed to heterosexual from homosexual and that he was now happily married. The other argued that therapy had no effect on him whatsoever and he that had the same homosexual orientation after treatment as he had before.

From a clinical point of view, these individuals were describing two different entities. There are biological and psychological factors that go into producing sexual orientation. There can be heavy genetic loading that leaves an individual with little or no sexual interest in the opposite sex. There can be heavy psychological loading with similar results. The problem lies in trying to determine how much nature and how much nurture (or lack thereof) will be involved in one's sexual orientation, whether it be heterosexual, homosexual, or bisexual.

Whether the homosexual orientation is changeable and whether it is acceptable to the person possessing it are two entirely separate questions. It is usually considered not changeable if there is heavy genetic loading. Genetic loading is given by nature, like the color of our eyes. The best we can do is to name the quality properly, like blue or brown for eye color. Heavy psychological loading has to do with the cultural and family influences that have contributed to the sexual orientation. This will usually involve some negative attitudes toward parents of the opposite sex. A typical, but by no means exclusive, example is a dominating mother who may have wanted a girl instead of a boy and who unconsciously rejects her son. Another is a distant and cold father who conveys messages of disappointment in his son for a variety of conscious or unconscious reasons. Similar rejecting and controlling behaviors are seen in the family dynamics of female homosexuals. These dynamics can result in a child acquiring a sexual interest in members of the same sex. There may be some possibility for change if there is heavy psychological loading and the individual in question is conflicted about his or her sexual orientation. If an orientation stems from fantasies in which members of the opposite sex are frightening, or from memories of the opposite sex never being available or trustworthy, the possibility for change exists if these distortions as they apply to all potential sexual partners can be corrected. Cases of conversion are in the minority.

Whether homosexual orientation is acceptable to the person possessing it is always an important issue. For some it is always a stigma. For others it is something that they have learned to accept with some difficulty. For still others it is the way they were made and a source of pride. There has been much more self-acceptance as the societal attitudes toward homosexuals have changed.

If a homosexual feels that the orientation is immutable, but not acceptable, and has given serious reflection to the issue, she might indeed need help in accepting who she is. If a homosexual is dissatisfied being homosexual and there is evidence that he may have heavy psychological loading in his background, a trial of therapy might be of value. If the individuals are able to convert, they will be happier, but if they cannot despite wishes and efforts to do so, they will need help in appreciating the efforts that have been made and be encouraged to accept their orientation as a given. This is similar to the way in which those with heavy genetic loading either accept their orientation or need help in accepting it if they cannot do so on their own. It needs also to be stated explicitly that no one can change his or her orientation without the desire to do so, and even that may not be enough. But it is a minimum starting point for those who wish to attempt the conversion.

Kelly was a twenty-year-old female hospitalized for depression. During the course of her hospitalization it came up that she had a homosexual relationship in place with which she was pretty comfortable. She also had an aversion toward all older men and would be hostile toward them for no apparent reason. She was much more tolerant of younger men, but not sexually attracted to them. When questioned in more detail about her sexual preferences, she was able to tell us that she had regular intercourse with her father from the age of nine to fourteen. She finally insisted that her father stop it and he did. Her mother was like a nonentity in the family.

One concern I have is that adolescents may be encouraged to accept homosexuality prematurely when it is more of a developmental issue for them and phase appropriate. Adolescents are in the process of discovering their sexual identities, and a homosexual inclination may be quite normal when it occurs only for a period of time and is not firmly fixed. Adolescents need to be given time and often need some skillful questioning to help them determine more accurately the nature of their homosexual interest. Again, a similar situation can exist for older adults who have a delayed psychosexual development and need to be treated as adolescents even though they are much older chronologically. This is especially true for those who have been sequestered in religious life and have had an almost exclusive exposure to members of the same sex. Only the details of cases can help to make the diagnosis as to just what type of homosexuality exists.

Some married people are homosexual, have sexual relations, and even have children. In the case of the male, he may be bisexual or use homosexual fantasies that are stimulating to him in the process of sexual relations with his wife. Although he is making love to a woman, in his imagination he is really making love to a man. This situation can lead to marital difficulties in a variety of ways. If the man confesses his images to his wife she may become disturbed. If the man desires to make the fantasies come true, he may start overt homosexual relationships of which his wife becomes aware or he may confess to her what is really going on and announce his intention to get out of the marriage. Diocesan marriage tribunals are familiar with such cases. Of course, homosexual women can likewise have entered into heterosexual marriages, have children, and finally realize that the object of their dreams is someone of the same sex. Bisexual individuals can also enter into these kinds of struggles with the recognition that even though there is an attraction to both sexes, there is a clear preference for same-sex individuals.

The church officially teaches that homosexual acts are intrinsically evil and that a homosexual inclination is an objective disorder. The U.S. Catholic bishops, in a draft of their pastoral letter "Always Our Children," taught that homogenital behavior is objectively immoral and distinguished between actions or behavior and orientation, which they appreciate as a given (and not a matter of choice and therefore not a matter of sin). However, when this draft was corrected by the Vatican's Congregation for the Doctrine of the Faith (CDF), the bishops issued a revised working document stating that homosexuality is "objectively disordered." This would seem to leave some ambiguity about the stance of the Catholic bishops and the Vatican regarding orientation or homosexual inclination.

The "intrinsically evil" concept was not used by the bishops but is clearly stated by the Vatican. This again is a throwback to a morality that considers an act in itself and away from a morality that considers the person performing the act. It bases morality on the very constricted order of nature rather than the broader and more inclusive order of reason. It shows a prejudice by which sexual ethics are treated very differently from social ethics and seems to ignore science, culture, and compassion.

It is important to consider the psychological effects of such teachings on the persons who struggle with these issues. If individuals are taught that a homosexual inclination is an objective disorder, and they recognize that they possess such an inclination, it is no longer objective because they possess it. It is a subjective disorder. It is a part of their being. It is not simply an inclination, like the seven capital sins, where one can see a tendency to do something wrong but no judgment is made of the inclination itself. Individuals can repress or deny homosexual inclinations, but they will probably emerge at a later date and bring havoc into the person's life. To be told that we have an objective disorder in our souls does not foster self-esteem nor respect or love for the one who tells us that. I would think that the more likely outcome for a healthy individual would not be acceptance, but loss of credibility in the teaching.

Courage is a Catholic organization that tries to help homosexuals live according to church teachings. They try to build self-esteem by focusing on what one is like as a person, and they do not regard sexual orientation as an important factor in that respect. The organization called Dignity does not agree with church teachings about homosexuality and tries to encourage individuals to follow their informed consciences in sexual matters.

My overall impression is that there are certain individuals who are immutably homosexually oriented and that these individuals experience sexual longings as intensely as any heterosexual. The bishop's initial official position that homosexual orientation is acceptable was clearly a move in the right direction, but in my opinion it has left some questions unanswered. It is church teaching that celibacy is a charisma or special gift from God, and that by definition not all individuals are called to it. It is further stressed by several authors discussing the possibility of celibacy that there are certain attitudes that need to precede and accompany a celibate commitment. Primary among these is that people must be doing it freely and willingly for the love of God. They are freeing themselves for service to others and are to be totally available for an open and loving relationship with God and the human community. The authors stress that the sexual energy needs to be sublimated in a healthy and generative way in the service of others for celibacy to succeed. It is also stressed that celibates need to foster a very close relationship with God through prayer and meditation. This later requirement has been confirmed by many celibates that I have talked with who gave up their prayer life about the same time that they became sexually involved with someone either homosexually or heterosexually.

It will either have to be posited, then, that all homosexual individuals have this gift (since church teaching denies genital expression to them), which many of them do not believe or feel they have, or there needs to be some moral room made for them to live in a holy committed relationship that will allow for genital expression that can foster love and generativity in their lives. Those that I am familiar with simply do not possess the qualities that spiritual writers and official church teaching state are necessary for celibate living. I am sure that some of them do, but I would consider this as a special gift that has not been given to all.

Homophobia is a concept that merits our attention in this section. It is usually described as a fear of being with a homosexual, usually on the part of another male. This is often not experienced as a fear, but more as an aversion. One of my patients, after coming to grips with his homosexuality, decided to "come out" with some of his friends. He was afraid that they would reject him. His fear came partially true. While some could easily accept his disclosure and even congratulate him on his courage, a few were explicit in their intolerance of such a condition. They clearly rejected him and wanted nothing more to do with him if he was going to pursue the "homosexual lifestyle."

The next level of homophobia usually takes the form of gay bashing. This is often perpetuated by the use of terms like "queer," "faggot," "fruit" or other derogatory expressions, coupled at times with outright harassment and physical punishment. Studies show that often these harassing individuals have an unconscious fear of their own homosexual tendencies, which have undergone various degrees of repression. The most tragic outcome of this attitude is when it leads to murder. There have been recent cases in the media of individuals being killed, often brutally, for no other reason than their homosexuality. One recent case saw a man being bludgeoned to death. He received repeated blows to his head and body, far beyond what was needed to kill him. It was construed as the murderer's desire to vent his hostility until it was spent. Further investigation revealed that the murderer had been involved in homosexual activities, which he hated. It was as if he were trying to punish his victim for the tendencies that he himself possessed and for behaviors in which he himself had likewise engaged.

Chapter 7

Sexuality, Contraception, and Reproduction

Mary was a thirty-eight-year-old woman who had been married since she was eighteen and had seven children. She came seeking help because she was very depressed. Her marriage was in trouble, and she wanted to be a good Catholic. For her being a good Catholic meant that neither birth control nor divorce were options. Feeling completely controlled by both parents, she entered marriage as a way of getting away from her family. She loved her husband, but she understood very little about sex or sexuality except that all forms of sex were to be avoided until marriage, and then everything was supposed to be somehow in order. To her disillusionment this was not the case at all. From the very beginning she found intercourse painful and had no desire for it. However, she felt some obligation to her husband, who was very interested in having sex. He initially tried to reassure her that sexual desire would come and was patient with attempts at arousal. But as the pregnancies and children came along, she lost whatever initial interest in sex he had been able to stimulate in her. Both began to doubt that she would overcome her frigidity.

I would be the first to say that there are large families in which the children and parents do very well and the children seem to thrive. There seems to be enough love for everyone, the children are industrious and successful, and the parents have enough energy and money to keep things going. I would also be the first to say that not all of us are capable of having and supporting a very large family, financially or emotionally. There are also women whose obstetrical histories are so marked by miscarriages and the consequent psychological trauma that it is imperative for their mental health that there be a strict control over future pregnancies.

Mary was a classical case of a well-intentioned young woman who with her husband was trying to live up to the strict precepts of the church as they saw them, causing considerable damage. Their entire marriage was unhappy, and after twelve years and seven children, they got a divorce. She continued raising the children, and he supported them, but there were constant recriminations on both sides: "If you had not gotten me pregnant so often...," and, "If you had not been so frigid...." Any couple therapist is very familiar with these scenarios. They are very difficult to treat, and sometimes they can't be treated for a variety of reasons.

Several years after their divorce, they managed to procure an annulment. Mary did not remarry, and she felt saddled with the children. Her husband did remarry. I always think of this couple's situation when I hear of young people entering into marriage where there is considerable psychosexual immaturity and naiveté about the consequences of pregnancies. This is a very important area for education, which can certainly include official church teachings. But there is a need for considerable input from pastoral counselors who are open to a couple's need for perspective on birth control or divorce, as well as input from psychologists who can help couples see beyond the dreaminess of "being in love."

Paula and Robert had been married for four years. They had two children ages one and three. They wanted their first child and took no precautions against the first pregnancy. They attempted to avoid the second child by practicing abstinence during Paula's fertile periods, but she became pregnant anyway. Both were afraid of another pregnancy for several reasons. Their finances were being stretched, and they were both already working. They had hopes for a college education for both children and felt the need to start saving for those expenses immediately as well as to begin saving for retirement. Robert had an elderly mother who required some financial help as well.

Paula decided to speak to the young assistant pastor in their parish when she went to confession. She asked if, given her circumstances, she and her husband could practice some form of artificial contraception. He rather abruptly pointed out that the church's position on the matter was very clear: only sexual activities in which the seed is deposited in the vagina with ejaculation, without any artificial means that could inhibit pregnancy, are permissible.

This began to cause Paula added concern. She and her husband had performed fellatio and cunnilingus at times when they did not have intercourse, and there were indeed times that ejaculations did not end up in her vagina. At times when she did not want to have intercourse, Robert was happy if she would masturbate him. After hearing what the priest said about official church teachings, she began to wonder if these practices were also wrong for a married couple, in general, even if they were not being used as a means of birth control. Robert, who was Jewish, had been tolerant of the whole natural family planning theory. He became less tolerant as the frustration of his sexual needs seemed to be increasing. When Paula told him what the priest had said, he became furious and expressed in no uncertain terms that he felt the priest had no business in their bedroom. Fortunately, Paula sought further help from her pastor, who skillfully managed to help her form her own conscience on the matter.

As already noted, the church teaches that the procreative and the unitive parts of marriage are of equal importance. Marriage is a lifelong commitment for the purpose of having children and raising and educating them, and for the mutual love, support, and sexual satisfaction of the spouses. The teaching also states that each act of sexual intercourse is to be open to both purposes and that nothing artificial should prevent conception or interfere with the love expressed by the partners in their mutual gift of self to the other. It is hard to improve on this Catholic ideal of marriage, but that is precisely one of its problems. It is an ideal, and we do not live in an ideal world.

When a couple is deeply in love, they wish to be psychologically and physically intimate. They do not want any barriers between them. The lyric line from "The Wedding Song, There is Love" expresses this openness: "a woman draws her life from man and gives it back again." The life referred to is both the vitality that they feel from being in love and the new life of pregnancy. They are committed to the relationship and open to having a child. Intercourse is freely and passionately undertaken. They really do desire to become one flesh, and at the moment of climax, the ejaculation is deeply deposited inside the woman's vagina. She longs for this moment and for the child that may result. The man wishes to satisfy her desires and is willing to provide for her as well as their child. Lovemaking under these circumstances is as good as it gets.

However, lovemaking is often not this good. If there are already children and worries about their care and education, both partners may be fearful of further procreation. If a woman has had miscarriages from which she is still recovering, she may need more time before she can risk another pregnancy. She may be very much in need of her husband's love and sexual intimacy to help restore her damaged sense of self and reassure her that she is still loved. If natural family planning methods work in such situations, and the woman has confidence in them, so much the better.

Natural family planning is often seen incorrectly, even by physicians, as the old calendar, temperature, and "rhythm" method. Rather, it is based on the findings of Doctors John and Evelyn Billings, that a woman's vaginal mucus serves as a reliable indicator of the hormonal changes that occur at the time of ovulation. This method can be used to either avoid a pregnancy or to create one, depending upon a couple's choice and appropriate use of the fertile periods.

Gerald Coleman in *Human Sexuality: An All Embracing Gift* summarizes their findings as follows:

1. The menstrual period at the start of each cycle is considered to be fertile. The reason for viewing the time of menstruation as fertile is that if a woman should have an unusually or unexpectedly short cycle such that the ovulation process were to begin toward the end of menstruation, she would have no warning of this fact since the presence of the menstrual flow would make it difficult for her to examine her vaginal mucus. Thus, as a precaution, women are advised to regard the menstrual period as fertile.

2. After menstruation, there is a noticeable absence of any vaginal discharge of mucus, and a woman experiences a definite sensation of dryness. During these days of dryness, the woman is infertile.

3. At the conclusion of this period of dryness, cervical mucus begins to be discharged from the vagina. At first, this mucus is a kind of cloudy, sticky discharge, but it gradually becomes a clear, egg-white, stretchy, and lubricative substance. The "peak" or main sign of ovulation is the last day on which this clear and stretchy mucus

is present. The women's period of fertility, however, is defined as starting with the first day of the cloudy mucus discharge and continuing up until three days past the peak symptom of ovulation.

4. From the fourth day after the peak symptom until the start of the next menstrual cycle, a period of infertility occurs.[30]

This method has certain pros and cons that need to be considered. Its main advantage is that it is "natural." Women often appreciate that they do not have to put any chemical or mechanical device in their bodies. It can be a problem for women who do not wish to be examining their vaginal secretions, and in countries where hygiene is poor, it may be difficult to accurately track the mucus cycle. The so-called period of "dryness" may not be so dry if a woman is sexually excited and lubricates in response to stimulation. There is considerable abstinence required to avoid a pregnancy, which can be difficult for newly married couples having intercourse two or three times per week. If the couple is highly motivated and can practice such restraint, their times of union can be more exciting and there is less chance of a dull sexual routine developing. On the other hand if the couple does not exercise the required restraint, there can be an unwanted pregnancy with serious consequences to the relationship. For some women, a simple injection once a month is the easiest way of taking care of the whole matter.

Artificial means of conception are not desirable in themselves and frequently reduce the pleasure of intercourse. However, a high degree of confidence in whatever method is used is very important for both partners, particularly the woman. Not to be respectful of her state of mind and her fear of an unwelcome pregnancy can hardly be considered lovemaking. A gift of love that is feared and unwelcomed is not a gift at all.

Situations like these require a great deal of communication between the spouses. They need to appreciate that they may be married for a long time and that their love life deserves the utmost care. Otherwise, sexual dysfunctions can arise that are very destructive to a marriage. Both partners need to be at the helm, guiding their ship through rough waters. More than one marriage has hit the birth control iceberg and been damaged by it, sometimes irreparably. Lovemaking that does not take into consideration all aspects of a couple's life together cannot be true love. It is paramount to consider that the couple's sexual life is fundamental to the preservation of the family unit. The couple's love life, which also means the love life of the family and its continuing stability for the children who may already be in their lives, cannot afford to take a back seat to methods of controlling pregnancy.

The shift from an action-centered to a person-centered morality allows for more consideration to be given to the child that results from a conception. This topic has not received enough attention based upon people's experiences. It is well accepted in psychology that a rejecting mother will not be able to adequately nurture her child. An unwanted pregnancy can certainly contribute to the mother developing a rejecting attitude.

One of the tragedies of the rigid application of the church's teaching on the purposes of marriage is that it will often turn the couple off to hearing the true beauty in the doctrine and using it as an ideal. It may even drive them away from the sacraments or out of the church altogether. It would seem to be time now for a different formulation of the doctrine which is forcing those doing pastoral care to frequently support couples in forming their own personal consciences against the church's formal teaching. With over 80 percent of Catholics practicing some form of artificial contraception, according to polls, the Spirit might be sending another message. Some might ask if the faith development of the couple and their use of prayer and sacraments is mature enough to allow them to follow the formal teaching. Others might ask if it is mature enough to allow them to differ.

One of the most depressing and, I am sorry to say, misguiding arguments that I have read about the official Catholic teaching and the use of condoms was reported by Thomas Fox in his excellent book *Sexuality and Catholicism:*

> At a 1988 Vatican conference on AIDS, a top church spokesman gave an example of the incredible lengths to which legalistic defenders of papal policy will go. Monsignor Carlo Caffara, dean of the Vatican's Institute on Marriage and Family Studies, said that if one spouse has AIDS, the couple must practice total abstinence. But if such abstinence might lead to adultery or grave harm to

conjugal peace, the couple may licitly have unprotected sex and risk infection.[31]

What is not addressed is that while trying to preserve one of the ends of marriage, having marital acts open to conception, the other and equally important end of marriage is being violated, the mutual love and support of the spouse. There is no way to imagine "conjugal peace" when one party is performing a potentially lethal act against the other. Even one unprotected sexual act with an infected person can lead to acquiring the deadly disease and months of uncertainty before knowing whether one is infected or not. Obviously the risk increases with each repeated act.

Countries where there is still considerable male dominance and little respect for women will be the most vulnerable to this attitude. Women in such situations are poor in almost every sense of the word. I cannot help but think that the mandates from Christ himself for preferential treatment for the poor would apply to them.

While entering a library to review the reference I am about to mention, I noticed the inscription "Omnia Vincit Veritas" carved in the store archway over the entrance After searching my memory for traces of high school Latin I came up with an approximate translation: "Truth Will Conquer Everything." It struck me as particularly pertinent because I was seeking an article in *America* magazine entitled "Tolerant Signals: The Vatican's New Insights on Condoms for H.I.V. Prevention."[32] The article carefully states that while much of the official position about condoms was unchanged, a spokesperson for the Vatican made a distinction between "prevention (attacking a problem at its roots) and containment (interventions that lessen the impact of a problem). The sense seemed to be that the use of condoms for containment is permissible as the "lesser of evils."

Even with considerable nuancing, there did seem to be some shift in perspective: behavior that was considered "intrinsically evil" (never objectively justifiable) was now considered "the lesser of evils" (somewhat justifiable). It seemed to imply that consideration for existing human life was as important as potential life. I could not help but wonder if a similar process in church thinking might have taken place with the issues of slavery, usury, the nature of the earth, and evolution. Stances in all four were radically reversed, but there must have been small cracks in the defensive structures before they collapsed, as well they should have.

THERE IS PROBABLY NOTHING more damaging to her sense of self-esteem than for a woman who desires to have a child not to be able to do so. It seems to go right to the core of her being and causes profound feelings of sadness and depression.

Stuart and Tracy present this kind of a problem. They had been married for several years and had been trying to have a child for most of that time. They underwent every possible test to determine the cause of the infertility, and none was found. Attempts at physically placing Stuart's sperm, which had an adequate count, directly into Tracy's vagina were not successful. She did not respond to the drugs that increase fertility, and she miscarried with *in vitro* fertilization. Finally it was suggested that she consider using a surrogate, and her sister who had no trouble with pregnancies volunteered. A dozen eggs were harvested from Tracy. All twelve were fertilized with Stuart's sperm. Of the six that took, three were placed in Tracy's sister, and the other three were placed in Tracy on the outside possibility that she might become pregnant and carry, even though she had miscarried with the *in vitro* procedure. Miracle of miracles, both women each delivered a healthy baby and Stuart and Tracy ended up with two infants.

Roberta is a fifty-year-old schoolteacher who has never been married. She has always wanted to have a child of her own but felt it was just not going to be possible. When she found out that a woman who is healthy and has a good life expectancy may well be able to carry a baby with both the sperm and the ovum being donated, she decided on the procedure. It was successful and she delivered a healthy baby girl without any complications.

It has recently been discovered that women can freeze their eggs and plan for a later pregnancy if they face the possibility of not being able to conceive because of advancing age without a partner or because some medical condition will require the removal of their ovaries.

I present these examples as raising the kind of questions regarding reproduction that are going to become more common as time goes on and specialized reproductive methods are perfected and become more popular. This of course is an ethical minefield, and I would not begin to go into all of the ethical questions and theological nuancing necessary to fully explore these problems. I would simply like to raise some issues for consideration and inquiry particularly from the psychological point of view.

The technology in these examples is rejected outright by the Magisterium cause it strikes at the meaning of sexuality and marriage as taught by the church.

According to current church teaching, obtaining the sperm through masturbation is considered intrinsically evil. Fertilizing ova with sperm outside of the uterus is considered to be immoral, particularly if some need to be discarded (officially a form of abortion). Surrogacy is also questioned in official teaching, because, according to this view, it goes against the integrity of the couple's union. I do not believe that there is any possibility for ethical progress in this area as long as an action-centered and not a person-centered approach is taken. Debating the morality of masturbation will carry little meaning for the potential parents of a child considering the seriousness of the medical problem that they are trying to solve.

If we start with a person-centered morality, we will normally find two people who have undergone considerable pain in trying to have a child in the unusual ways. They have had extensive medical testing, sometimes surgery, have been disappointed either by an inability to conceive or repeated miscarriages, and often have seriously considered adoption. What these couples feel, and it is usually the woman who understandably has the stronger opinion, is that they want to have a biological child of their own. At times it is the woman's most deeply felt need.

The main objection raised by the Magisterium to fostering a person-oriented approach to these moral matters is that it is intrusive to both the love and reproductive aspects of marriage to have such artificial interventions occur, and therefore it is not permissible. I can only comment by trying to recount the feelings of one woman whom I discussed these procedures with in great detail. She felt that she and her husband would not want any outside help or intrusion in conceiving a baby if they could do it on their own. She could give a very vivid account of what it was like to be thoroughly invaded by medical procedures, not just once but on a regular basis, including pelvic examinations, sonograms to track ovulations, and repeated blood withdrawals. This was in addition to feeling that her body was not her own because it had been so altered by chemicals to prepare her for ovulation enhancement. Given the uncertainty of success, not to mention the expense, which is into the thousands of dollars, she wondered whether any reasonable person would go through these procedures and whether it made sense ethically or otherwise. Her conclusion was always that there is nothing more important to her than having a child of her own. Creating life was her number one priority, even with considerable discomfort to herself and anxiety for her husband.

Discarding a fertilized ovum officially is a form of abortion in church eyes. I would suggest that discarding a fertilized ovum prior to implantation may differ from a true pregnancy. Nature discards fertilized ova herself. An ovum can be fertilized in the fallopian tube and never implanted in the uterine wall. (It becomes another ethical issue to remove an implanted fertilized ovum because of the fear of too many pregnancies going to term.)

There is a world of difference between discarding a fertilized ovum from a test tube, and to take an extreme example, sucking the brains out of an infant after it has been partially born (the so-called "partial birth abortion.") Conservatives make no such distinction.

It is officially taught that the moment of fertilization is also the moment of conception. A fertilized ovum can exist in the fallopian tube for several hours before it is implanted in the uterine wall. I would argue that the implantation is what makes the conception. A fertilized ovum in a test tube can be discarded without implantation. When implantation occurs the pregnancy is truly underway and will be terminated only by a spontaneous or an artificial abortion. A fertilized ovum in a test tube before conception is only a few hours into existence without any real differentiated parts. A child partially born is ready for independent existence with well developed and completely differentiated parts.

The pro-life rational argument here is this: the one-cell, newly fertilized ovum is a new human different only in age and location from an older adult, but existing in a test tube. The element of truth in this can blur the fact that there will very likely be no fully formed human beings from these one-cell organisms if selection of healthier fertilized ova for implantation is not made by humans. There will be no children receiving love from parents who desperately want them and are capable of real love and care for them, and no grandparents delighted with their existence. I must question whether the pro-life advocates in these circumstances are pro-life or pro-principle. The usual way of expressing the pro-life position is to affirm that human life is to be valued from the first moment of conception until death. The primary definition of conception is the formation of a zygote capable of survival and maturation in normal conditions. The secondary definition is the entity so formed, an embryo, a zygote. Everyone would have to agree that an artificially fertilized ovum prior to implantation is not capable of survival. "Normal" implies that the fertilized ovum be implanted in the uterus before there is a conception.

Some will suggest that women who cannot have their own biological children should adopt. Many of them do and are very grateful for this blessing in their lives. There are others who feel that being a biological mother is what matters, and they will not choose adoption as long as medical science offers them some hope of having their own child.

Another interesting phenomenon that the situation of Stuart and Tracy might illustrate is the unknown effect of an existing child on the pregnancy process. It is common for women believing they cannot have children to adopt and subsequently conceive and have a child of their own. This phenomenon is not understood, but it is certainly no surprise. In this case we could only wonder if Tracy's successful pregnancy was influenced by the knowledge that her sister was carrying her child.

Part III

Practical Questions

Chapter 8

Sexuality and Spirituality

I consider this chapter the most important one in the book because it deals with our destiny as human beings. St. Augustine said it so well centuries ago in his *Confessions:* "Our hearts are restless, O Lord, until they rest in Thee." We need not look very far to find evidence of restlessness. We are rushing everywhere. New terms have even been coined, and we have enacted laws dealing with "road rage" and "aggressive driving." Restaurants increasing load the plates with more food than people can eat. We are a hungry people, but I do not believe that our hunger is just for food. Our television programs have as many as ten commercials during each break to offer more and more things that we simply must have. We move in and out of committed relationships so often that someone recently described it as "serial monogamy." Is this the ideal for the future? It would imply that while we need to be committed to just one person at a time, it need not be for life. Are we losing the ideal "until death do us part?" Hopefully that is not happening. We indeed have restless hearts.

At the outset, I cited the definition of sexuality presented in a document by the bishops which reads as follows: Sexuality is "a fundamental component of personality in and through which we, as male and female, experience our relatedness to self, others, the world, and even God." The "even God" part denotes spirituality: our energies and capacities to relate to God. Another part of spirituality not included in our natural definition is the grace that God provides. "Grace builds on nature" has been a well-accepted principle in theology. We try to understand and control nature, but God provides graces that are beyond our comprehension.

Spirituality concerns our relationship — natural and supernatural — with that Higher Power who can satisfy our restless hearts and our insatiable longings. For monotheists this Higher Power is God. For

115

Christians it is a God who unequivocally loves us and sent his Son, Jesus, for our redemption guided by the Holy Spirit. For Hindus it is belief in a supreme being of many forms, reincarnation, and the desire to be liberated from earthly evils. For Buddhists it is the belief that suffering and existence go together. They hope that if the self with its senses can become extinguished one will reach a state of illumination beyond both suffering and existence. For some it is a belief in a Power outside of themselves because they have conceded they do not have the power to control themselves.

Spirituality is not a system of beliefs. That is what a religion is. But spirituality is most certainly based on beliefs. Spirituality is relating to and communicating with that Higher Power, however the divine is regarded in our lives. It can be something as casual as an occasional marvel at the mystery of our existence as we contemplate a sunrise or the stars of our universe. It can be something all-consuming of our energies and dedications. God is always totally available. All spiritualities have practices or rituals which are used to elicit the desired result of this divine connection. Very prominent among these practices are sacred space and sacred rituals, silence, meditation, and contemplation.

In the past, trying to mix sexuality and spirituality has been like trying to mix oil and water. Obviously the ancients were coming from a different place. Spirituality had no part in their definition of sexuality. If there were ever attempts to mix them, the dualism of the past would quickly separate them again. In the past, to be spiritual was not to be sexual, and to be sexual was not to be spiritual. The flesh was to be denied, beaten, and crucified that the spirit might live. I do not mean to imply that there is no longer a need for discipline and restraint in the spiritual life. What I hope we are coming to, though, is the ability to see sexuality as a dye added to the water of spirituality that permeates and adds to its beauty. The identity of each will be changed by the proper fusion with the other. We need a spirituality that fits our sexuality, and a sexuality that fits our spirituality. I hope we are coming to see that flesh and spirit can flourish together simply because they are both created by God, and they need to be fused in the Presence of God.

In this chapter I would like to explore how sexuality and spirituality might become better fused or integrated. The essence of this fusion-integration is for these aspects of ourselves to come face to face with each other in the Presence of God. This is not always easy, as we will see, but it is also not impossible. I would like to approach it by considering the basic tools that we possess in each area to help us with the process. For spirituality it is prayer. For sexuality it is self-reflection. No one has grown in either area without employing these instrumentalities, and each has several aspects that require discussion. (I might mention parenthetically that help with prayer is often sought from a spiritual director, while help with self-reflection is often sought from a therapist or counselor.) In considering several aspects of each separately, it will become clearer how the integration can take place.

Before proceeding any further I would like to offer two cases that might illustrate what results when integration of the spiritual and the sexual does not take place.

Vernon came to me in his early forties. He was considered a rising star in the diocesan priesthood. He was unable to complete a graduate degree after having done very well academically in the previous years. He was beginning to become preoccupied with sexual fantasies which he had given no more then a fleeting thought in the past. He had regarded them as sinful and dismissed them. He had entered the seminary at a very early age and had never masturbated or dated. He always felt that his body was an occasion of sin and even had trouble looking at his genitals or washing them.

Freud says the way we deal with our bodies will often become the way we deal with our minds, and I must say that I have never seen a better example. Vernon's inhibitions to engage himself physically and psychologically finally resulted in his inability to engage himself intellectually, which resulted in a professional and vocational disaster. This is a priest who had spent many hours in meditation and had frequent access to spiritual direction, but somehow never could see himself as a total human being in the presence of the God he loved so much.

Sister Rose was a thirty-five-year-old woman who came to me because of increasing fatigue and depression. She was the oldest of seven children and recalled much of her childhood as a time she spent taking care of her younger siblings in order to help her mother (who herself was chronically fatigued, depressed, and frequently pregnant). She was very dedicated to her family, but also felt the need to be away from them. She began to see that going into the convent was a way of ensuring that she would not have children of her own, and that she could feel worthwhile by devoting herself to others as she had learned to do so well in her family. Her problems arose when she started a casual acquaintance with an inactive priest who worked in the same facility. They went through all of the steps of intimacy described earlier, but when it came to the point where they both started gratifying some of their mutual wishes for physical contact, conflicts began. For the longest time, they avoided actual intercourse, because it seemed inappropriate, but there was much satisfaction in foreplay. Once they started having intercourse it became obvious to them that they had become just like a married couple without actually living together. However, getting married was a problem for the priest because he was still under vows. Sister Rose had come to realize that she needed someone in her life who could reciprocate love. This led to her leaving the convent, but she still had doubts about marriage, because in her mind it meant having children. The extent of the denial of her sexuality was typical of many who spent years of meditation and prayer in the convent. Her sexuality never became integrated with her vowed celibacy.

Let us now consider prayer and self-reflection in more detail.

Prayer is essentially our communication with God. It involves formal prayers (such as saying the Lord's prayer) or attending religious services. Religious writers through the years have considered the two forms of prayer known as living in the Presence of God and meditation to be essential for spiritual progress.

Living in the Presence refers to acquiring the habit of turning our attention to God, often saying a short prayer, but mainly just trying to have a sense of God's presence. It reminds me of the state of mind that is spontaneously acquired when we fall in love, particularly in the early stage referred to as infatuation. The newly found love is always on our minds. We can do a variety of things, many times quite happily, with a simultaneous awareness of the loved one's existence. That person is never very far from our minds.

As we start to live in the Presence, our lives begin to change. We begin to view everything that we are, have, and do in the light of this Loving Presence. Everything has its meaning insofar as it fosters or detracts from the pursuit of living in the Presence. Our sexual side and our spiritual side circle ever closer together as we see them coming from the same Creator and their inherent goodness shines through. Our sexuality and spirituality can become only connected through our awareness, and now this awareness is permeated with a sense of the Divine.

God not only created us so that we would grow through psychosexual development; God is also there to assist with the many struggles that confront us during that development. The seven capital sins are not nearly so powerful when we view them in the Divine Presence and have a sense of divine grace. Our imperfect knowledge about our sexuality, psychology, and theology is not as terrifying if we consider that the Spirit will bring to our minds all things that we need for successfully living our lives when they are motivated by love.

Many fine books on prayer are available today. I would simply like to briefly describe one of the oldest and best-known forms of prayer started many centuries ago by St. Benedict in order to give some context to the notion of meditation. St. Benedict spoke of *lectio divina,* reading the word of God, as the way to begin prayer. It later was broadened to include any inspiring reading suitable for the beginning prayer. One reads along until one is struck by a particularly meaningful passage. Once that sense of importance is experienced it is recommended that the person pause and begin to repeat the passage slowly over and over again. As this is done the individual will begin to have further thoughts and emotional reactions and be inclined to express these emotions to God. This is the step known as meditation. It recommended to continue comfortably with this reflection as long as one is inclined. After whatever potential was there seems to have been exhausted, then the process of reading, repeating, and meditation is entered into again. There is one further step that occurs by the grace of God with some people during the process of meditation: being completely consumed with the sense of the Divine Presence and wishing to let go of all else in order to experience it fully. This is referred to as contemplation. If this occurs there is no need to return to the earlier steps for as long as it continues.

Self-reflection is the unique capacity that we humans possess to examine our behaviors and guide our choices. Self-reflection about our progress through the stages of psychosexual development is essential for all of us. It doesn't often occur in a formal manner, or even with knowledge that the stages of psychosexual development exist, but we can examine our lives and personal growth using our common sense and see whether we are maturing or remaining immature. (As a matter of fact we even have talk shows these days which help us with it.) But it does require that we have the interest in such a pursuit. And it can be said for most of us that there are times when we do not have such an interest.

One way to help illustrate this self-reflective capacity is to consider some of the principles of psychoanalysis. Psychoanalysis itself as a form of treatment is not common or necessary for many, but as a discipline it has taught us a considerable amount about how the mind works, and that is universally helpful. It is with this in mind that I will review some important analytic concepts that clearly deal with our personal development and that can be shown to have spiritual overtones as well. The issues I will consider are free association, transference, and resistance. Once these are described in more detail it might be easier to see their application to our self-reflection and their role in our psychological growth and integration with our spirituality. It can be said at the outset that when meditation involves self-reflection on sexuality in the Presence of God, the process of integration is underway.

Turning our attention now to some of the principles that analysis has to offer, we can say that psychoanalysis begins when a child first starts to wonder about things going on inside. There are feelings to be named, thoughts to be sorted out, and motivations to be understood. Much of this goes on without the child paying attention to what is developing, but even a two- or three-year-old can ask an endless series of questions. At some age, we recognize our capacity to reflect upon ourselves as well as the world.

As this self-reflective capacity grows, we can continue to develop it independently over many years and acquire considerable self-knowledge. In many cases, things start to get confusing, conflicts develop, and we experience psychic pain and often other psychic symptoms. This can prompt us to tell our feelings to family members or close friends in order to help cope with them. Sometimes we may even be inclined to seek therapy or counseling. Because so many therapies are based on the analytic model, I will describe a little about the analytic process itself to demonstrate how developing awareness and self-reflection take place. Again there may be modifications of this method depending upon the therapist and the goals that are set for the treatment. The fundamental dynamics sought in most of these therapies have to do with developing an increasing awareness or consciousness of what is going on in us mentally through the process of free association.

Free association can best be understood by looking at how it is practiced in classical analysis. Classic psychoanalysis requires certain tasks of the analyst and certain tasks of the subject. Individuals undergoing analysis must agree to say whatever comes to mind without the usual screening of what seems irrelevant, unimportant, or embarrassing. They must agree to attend frequent sessions at regular times and pay a fee in accordance with their means. Analysts listen to the flow of associations and then point out whatever they think might be relevantly connected. The subjects are then in a position to react to whatever is said with whatever comes to mind. This simple process can have profound and far-reaching effects when carried out faithfully over a period of time on suitable individuals and with properly trained therapists. It brings the unconscious and preconscious to consciousness and tells us a great deal about how our minds work. As our awareness is enhanced, so are our choices and our abilities to make them.

Two important phenomena can occur during the course of analysis and therapy that are of particular importance in the integration of spirituality and sexuality. They are transference and resistance. Transference is part of our nature and refers to our tendency to regard persons in our present life with an attitude or feeling similar to an attitude or feeling that we had toward persons of significance in our past. The attitude or feeling can be positive or negative. It can be conscious, preconscious, or unconscious. These attitudes are acquired in the course of our psychosexual development and can be applied very automatically and often unconsciously to God. There is usually some basis in reality for the transference reaction, but its significance comes from its distortion.

A student may react toward a strict teacher like he or she did toward a strict father and may develop a defiant attitude expressed in silence, not working, or not paying attention. "Getting back" becomes even more important than learning, even at the price of self-defeat. God is sometimes seen as a strict parent. Defiance on our part may be the outcome, which will not foster spirituality and probably will not foster mental health either. If God is seen as a loving parent, we are much more apt to attempt an ongoing relationship that will foster our spiritual growth, similar to the way such an attitude fosters our natural growth.

As we grow spiritually we will review our preconceived notions of God and discard many distortions. Sometimes we can see God as a parent whom we can manipulate. We will show only what we think the parent will approve of and hide the rest. The only person who gets fooled with that kind of transference is ourselves. We can distort what is an appropriate feeling toward God, namely, reverence and awe, into a God who is terrifying and in whose Presence we must live in mortal fear, usually sacrificing some of our God-given freedom. We can also distort God into a parent who is so loving that no responsibility is demanded and hence we never have to grow up.

Once we become familiar with the concept of transference we can then begin to assess our reactions toward God with it in mind, particularly when we know something is true with our minds but our hearts lead us somewhere else. It is precisely with our concept of God and our struggles with sexuality that the "rubber hits the road" when it comes to integrating the two. If God is seen as punitive and nonaccepting of our sexual impulses, division begins to occur. If God is seen as a loving God and the creator of our sexuality, integration is the more likely outcome. There are obviously many images of God and many aspects of sexuality that can be examined. Another example that I have heard more than once is a person who is convinced that God is loving and trustworthy, but who is afraid to trust and let go. The need to stay in control really has more of a parental basis, like the fear of being dominated or abandoned, than anything to do with God. Such a God is really not going to be told much about our sexual selves.

An equally important concept is the notion of attachment. We might consider attachments as the basis for transference. Without some early relationship of significance there is no template for reactions, whether they be positive or negative, later in life. (The detachment disorder was described earlier. This is its opposite.) Freud spoke of cathexsis, which is defined as the emotional investment placed in someone or something. This emotional investment is crucial for proper development. I recently heard that there was a new rendition of the following popular saying with regard to Mary Magdalene: many things have been forgiven her because she has loved much. The newer version has it that she has been forgiven many things, therefore she has loved much. The latter really makes a lot more psychological sense. In our development, we are unlikely to do for others unless others have done for us first.

I recently had a very delightful experience with my twenty-two-month-old granddaughter. We were having an "ice cream party," and I was feeding her with a small spoon. At one point she redirected the spoon away from her mouth toward my own. She wanted me to take some ice cream from her even though I had some in front of me. So we began a fun game of one spoonful for her and one for me. She had learned sharing because she wanted not only to taste something good, but also to feel what she sensed as my delight in feeding her. This was not the first time she had done such a thing and was an example of transference occurring at a very early age.

The other phenomenon that analysis instructs us about is resistance. Basically it is our desire to keep things out of our awareness because they cause us anxiety or guilt when we think about them. *Resistance is probably the core that keeps spirituality and sexuality separated.* We can resist seeing our sexual impulses and fantasies. We can resist seeing our sexual orientation. We can resist seeing our sexual values and beliefs. We can resist seeing what effect our sexual behaviors have on others. We can resist making choices that will bring our sexual impulses and values more in conformity. We can resist seeing our sexuality as a divine gift. We can resist seeing our sexuality as good. If we are not able to break through resistances and be free with whatever associations come into our mind, we cannot develop either spiritually or sexually.

I would like to give a very simple personal example of resistance. It occurred in me while I was in a meditation group in which we shared different objects to meditate upon. I took a beautiful sea shell. I was holding it in my hand and stroking it. Suddenly I became uncomfortable and started to feel some anxiety. I wanted to turn my mind to something else without really knowing why. Anxiety is a sign of some danger being present that we have not yet clarified in our minds. I started to have some interesting associations after forcing myself to look further. The sea shell had a beautiful pink color, was very smooth to touch, and had a form similar to a woman's genitals. My fear was that during the sharing that goes on at the end of the meditation I would have to describe what I had been thinking about. I was afraid of being criticized, particularly because people knew that I was a psychiatrist, and everyone knows that psychiatrists have dirty minds! Once I got past that prejudice and gave others credit for being less judgmental, I could calmly describe my thoughts and give them an opportunity to appreciate the true beauty of the creation I was holding in my hands, including the explicit sexual overtones.

Perhaps we can now look at some of the overlap between meditation (or contemplative prayer) and self-reflection (or psychotherapy) in order to further appreciate how they are importantly related in the integration of our spirituality and sexuality.

During the course of our lives we might become graced by the desire to go deeply into our souls and come closer to the Ultimate Source of all things, the Ultimate Why. This is done through meditation and contemplative prayer as described earlier — a process whose initiation and proceedings, like those of analysis, are simple. We begin meditation by setting aside daily times for reflection in a conducive environment. We assume a body posture that will enhance relaxation and openness (as does reclining on the couch in analysis). There are various simple exercises or practices that are designed as tools to foster this openness: focusing on our breathing, thinking about a passage from Scripture, chanting a word or phrase, performing relaxation exercises, and listening to our bodies.

Once serious self-reflection or meditation has begun, some interesting things start to happen. Both processes are inner-directed and are often done with the help of another: In therapy, the other is the therapist; in meditation, the Other is God. Over time, both processes require a trust deep enough to expose our nakedness and a willingness to look at all that is there. This has been difficult for us since sin originated in the Garden of Eden and we felt the need to be clothed.

When we begin therapy, there are many things to recount about our life history and important relationships. At times we are surprisingly moved to tears as repressed memories emerge and old pains are recalled. When we begin mental prayer it is amazing how this same history takes on a new dimension as it is seen through God-illuminated eyes. Life becomes more meaningful as old values fade and new ones develop. Tears come with much relief, sometimes with and sometimes without an explanation. Often, there are associated feelings of gratitude, peace, forgiveness, and wonder at the providence of God.

One of the most striking similarities that I have experienced between analysis and contemplative prayer is that they both involve relating to someone who is not seen. After an initial evaluation and some discussion about the conditions for analysis, such as times of sessions, fees, and the need to say everything that comes to mind, the analyst invites the subject to lie on the couch while the analyst listens from a position behind the couch and out of the person's view. Once this is done, there is a very clear sense of the presence of someone who cannot be seen. The awareness of God's presence is very similar and likewise ushered in by certain preparations, such as lighting a candle, making the sign of the cross, or taking a few deep breaths. God and analyst become available to hear everything that we have to say and to see everything that we are.

The therapeutic situation is a very compassionate one. Hopefully we can create a similarly compassionate attitude when we are doing private reflection. They are really holding environments that allow a person to continue his or her growth which has been stymied for whatever reasons. The same can be said of spiritual direction. I am often reminded in this regard of the Scripture quote, "Be compassionate as God is compassionate" (Luke 6:36). The word "compassion" is related to the Aramaic word for "womb." Compassion is an outstanding quality of God and an essential ethical teaching of Jesus. Being in the Presence of God is being in the Presence of compassion personified, a womb-like holding environment for our continued spiritual growth.

A suggestion from the therapist or the spiritual director that we might wish to begin with an autobiographical sketch brings a little sense of direction and control into a situation that can otherwise be quite overwhelming. The interesting thing about this comparison is that neither the subject nor the therapist knows what is coming, but God does.

Before we go very far in either process, the flow of ideas and feelings that we can comfortably report or pray about begins to slow down. We notice that there are moments when revealing ourselves does not feel safe. We become resistant to carrying out the task of saying whatever comes to mind or thinking about certain things before God. What is feared is often not immediately clear (as in the personal example I cited above), but if pursued it will turn out to be something that we are projecting onto the therapist or God. This is how transference enters into the process. The subject may feel that the therapist is being silent or disinterested — or may imagine that the therapist is awestruck at the brilliance being witnessed! The therapist or God may be seen as a disapproving parent, particularly if sex is viewed as a shameful topic. God can be felt as One who is never there in times of need. We might miss a therapy session to avoid presumed shaming by the therapist, or we might avoid meditation because it never seems to be good enough or what God expects.

These projected positive or negative attitudes will be corrected over time as we become clearer about the reality of the helping person and the reality of God. As these resistances break down we become much freer mentally and spiritually.

One of the marvels of the human mind is that it can function very rapidly. Different trains of thought and feelings can occur simultaneously, which can cause a sense of conflict and confusion regarding what to talk about or what to pray about. When this happens in therapy, the therapist may suggest that it might be more useful to pursue what seems to be a more difficult line of feeling or thinking. When it happens in mental prayer, we might likewise choose to follow the more difficult line in God's presence. God already knows about it. It is a matter of our recognizing whatever it is we wish to avoid in God's presence. When it happens during private personal reflection, it is often useful to keep a journal. The process of writing whatever it is we are thinking about enables us to slow down long enough to record the issues and to sense more clearly the resistances. Sometimes we cannot even imagine writing these kinds of things down because we are afraid that someone might discover what we have written.

One further similarity between meditation and therapy is living in the moment. The therapist continually draws attention to what the subject is experiencing in the here and now. That may mean reporting a memory from the past, but the therapist may well be clarifying that the memory is being presently experienced. The implication is that it can be influenced in whatever direction the subject may choose. In meditation we strive to be aware of God's presence here and now and to be attentive to how anything else we might think or feel relates to that reality.

In the Fall 1999 *Shalem News*, Theresa Cavenaugh wrote an article entitled "Living in the Present."*[33] She describes how having an awareness of the moment, being engaged in what is before us, and devoting our energies to whatever that matter might be is a way of living in the presence of God. It is another version of Thich Nhat Hanh's "mindfulness" or the admonition of St. Ignatius to his Jesuit followers, "age quod agis, do what you do," or Anthony DeMello's "awareness, awareness, awareness."

The spiritual director and therapist have one very important belief in common. They rely on the innate capacity for development and do not try to unduly influence that capacity. The therapist knows that we have a capacity to appreciate and understand ourselves. It is developed over time by an identification with the therapist's tasks of listening carefully, making connections, and having a tolerance for viewing everything possible within our minds. This identification process is also part of the development of compassion toward ourselves, which I am sorry to say is often very lacking. The therapist also believes that developmental potential is always there and can be resumed at any time no matter where the patient might be stuck. The spiritual director knows that the Spirit is the true spiritual guide and tries to function in such a way as to allow the Spirit to direct. Spiritual growth is assured to anyone who seeks it. Jesus tells us to seek and we shall find. Knock and it will be opened to us.

With the posture of openness common to both therapy and meditation, there are many directions we can go toward understanding how the mind works or how we draw closer to God. After a while it becomes clear that we are following one of two forms of thinking or praying: we are either considering issues in the presence of the therapist or God, or we are focusing directly on the therapist or God. The former is particularly useful in seeing trends of associations or defense mechanisms, and the latter is particularly useful in dealing with transference distortions.

Considering issues gives us ample opportunity to review and work out all of the aspects of our psychosexual development and an opportunity for the spiritual integration that is necessary for all of us, whether celibate, married, or single. Focusing on the therapist gives us an opportunity to clarify many childish distortions in our thinking and feeling, while focusing on God is the beginning of contemplation as these distortions are eliminated.

Having described some of the similarities and differences between meditation and self-reflection or therapy, I would like to pursue some thoughts about meditation and contemplation. These terms also have

some overlap and are not always used according to their strict defini-
tions. Writers traditionally speak of meditation as being cataphatic or
apophatic. The former refers to a kind of thinking about many things in
God's presence, often starting with some reading from Scripture (*lectio
divina*) or other type of spiritual reading as described earlier to stimulate thinking and emotional responses; the latter refers to being aware
of God's presence in a loving way and trying to avoid thinking. There
is inevitable overlap regardless of which term is used.

The contemplative type of meditation is simply being content to be
in God's Presence and making attempts to keep everything else out of
mind so that our complete focus can be on God. We are much less
focused on the thoughts spontaneously going through our mind and in
fact try to let them pass by without much attention. This is very different
than seeing God as a partner helping us to view and understand what
is going on inside our minds and outside in our world. The significant
thing is that we are in relationship with God in either type.

I think that being very close to someone and being able to "hang
out" in silence is one of the most satisfying experiences we can have as
human beings. The other's presence is so real, yet nothing is expected.
There is no effort to be expended. I love the times when my wife and I
are sitting silently in our family room. We can be reading or snoozing or
meditating or just being. The fire is going and our dog, Abby, is lying in
front of it, also content with us and herself. (I sometimes wonder what
is going on in her mind, but she keeps that between herself and God!)

We need to be comfortable with both types of meditation because both are needed for psychosexual and spiritual growth. As just
one example, if we did not use our reflective minds we could avoid
understanding our sexuality and be vulnerable to the many things such
ignorance delivers on people. I would like to emphasize here that I am
not just referring to sexual aspects of ourselves, our genitality as such,
but to our sexuality in the broadest meaning of that term. We sometimes
need to struggle in God's presence to achieve that kind of understanding. If we are not open to this need, it becomes too easy to just push
thoughts aside that might be trying to tell us something about our sexuality and to rationalize it by saying we are practicing contemplation.
For example, we might find it more comfortable to be contemplative
and not face up to sexual orientation conflicts somewhere in our soul.

Likewise we can obsess about everything under the sun and not draw any closer to the God who made our soul, if we have a fear of intimacy for the many reasons that such a fear can exist.

So far we have considered transference and attachment (or cathexsis) as important ingredients in our relationships. I would like to add that attachment is not always a good thing, and in fact some forms of detachment can be beneficial and even necessary. (I am not speaking of the detachment disorder referred to earlier; that is always harmful.) Again we see virtue taking the middle ground. There is an important difference between what is considered attachment and what is considered an excessive attachment or enmeshment. Some examples of excessive attachments are a self-willfulness, a "my way or the highway" attitude, an excessive dependency as in a sycophant or some addictions such as to food, alcohol, or sex.

Christ spoke of detachment when he told one potential disciple to go sell what he had and to follow him. And he spoke of those who would not leave father or mother or brother or sister to follow him as being not worthy of him. Obviously, Christ was speaking not of some literal detachment from family but of the need to put God first in our priorities.

Many of the saints described how they detached themselves from the world, and in many cases how they tried to detach themselves from their bodies. There is a kind of detachment spoken of by St. John of the Cross and St. Teresa of Avila that leads to a dark night of the senses and a dark night of the soul. These are designed to free the spirit for *reattachment.* God of course is the first object of this new attachment, and subsequently all of the attachments of our lives derive their value as we see them more through God's eyes than our own. Our lives and possessions are seen more as belonging to God and simply on loan to us.

There is no question that children need to be attached to parents, and parents to children, for there to be life, growth, and health. But as time goes on, these attachments need to be scrutinized. What is appropriate attachment for an infant is not for a toddler; what is appropriate for a child is not appropriate for an adolescent; and what is appropriate for an adolescent is not appropriate for an adult. This might seem obvious, but as a matter of fact, it is surprising just how out of sync we parents can be with the chronological age of our children. Adolescents are perhaps the most forceful in reminding us of their need for independence. It is only after they have experienced this independence, and we parents have allowed them to experience it, that they are free to come back and be adults with us. There is a further kind of detachment which takes place when we see our children as God's most precious gifts, but nevertheless as God's gifts on loan to us.

The parents who are so attached to their adolescents that they refuse to set rules out of a fear of being disliked will do the adolescents a disservice. The adolescents will fail to develop proper boundaries and expect the world to always cater to their needs as the parents did. Parents who are overcontrolling and run a "tight ship" might have their adolescents jumping overboard in many different ways as time goes on.

I have often wondered about a kind of dualistic thinking that pervades the prayers and meditation of many religious sisters, brothers, and priests fostering a certain repression of their sexuality for so many years. If sexual thoughts, feelings, and impulses need to be repressed rather than considered in the presence of God, it might help explain why so many of these issues would not be brought up in self-reflection, meditation, and spiritual direction, only to emerge later in some form of crisis. I am reminded of a priest in his late fifties who was struggling to integrate a female friendship into his life. There were many positive aspects to their relationship, but there had been some sexual touching which he was determined to eliminate, but without success. I asked him in a way uncharacteristic for me as a therapist if he had considered his dilemma in the presence of God. He was absolutely astonished that I would ask such a question, and equally astonished that it had not occurred to him to do so.

The question is sometimes asked, "Can God remove one's sexual drive so that living a life of celibacy is not a struggle?" The simple answer is yes, because God can do anything. God is the author of nature and can modify it at will. But most celibates whom I have spoken with have not been so graced. There are more puzzling questions, however, that are not so easily answered. If we do not experience any, or very little, sexual drive, is that because of divine intervention? It is hard to say because we can have very little or no sexual drive by nature. But also in the course of development we can be so repressed in our sexuality that sexual impulses are minimum or even nonexistent. One can even feel called to celibacy because there is no real desire for marriage or intimate relationships. This can be from a combination of low biological urges and psychologically repressive mechanisms, often unconscious, which are long forgotten in their development. For some people this can be a fortuitous situation if they choose a religious life, and it encourages further repression of their sexuality. However, it can be a dangerous situation if their delayed sexuality, which might even have been considered as a special gift, suddenly emerges and leaves them in the midst of some adolescent struggle for control in their twenties — or sixties. I have seen examples from these age groups and all in between.

One of the very common manifestations of our restless hearts is "sexual addiction." When I trained as a psychiatrist this was not a diagnosis, or even a common behavior pattern, but today it is widespread. The sexual addict is someone whose main treasure in life is sex. This can include daily masturbation, with or without pornography, multiple partners, going to strip joints, and feeling an insatiable appetite for sex that is never satisfied but drives the addict to seek fulfillment time and time again. One particular facilitator today for the sexual addict's behavior is the Internet. There is a variety of sexually exciting websites that one can log on to, and it is available twenty-four hours a day, seven days a week, and in privacy. For many men that also means during work hours.

Women can also become sexual addicts, but the frequency for women is less, perhaps ten male addicts for every female addict. There is a basic difference in the way that men and women see sex, which may account for this contrast. Men are more likely to see sex as something they get. It is out there and needs to be sought. Young men will frequently wonder if somebody "got some," "got it," or "got a piece." Clearly, this is to see women as sexual objects. Women on the other hand are more relational and are more likely to wish to be loved, cherished, and fulfilled in motherhood. Women's longing is more to be loved, while the male longing is more for conquest. Interestingly enough, though, the underlying drive is the same, the emptiness which has not been filled. Judging from the amount of risk that the addict is willing to take to satisfy the addiction, this emptiness seems to be so much more intense for those who develop these behaviors. It is so intense that families, careers, and professions have been sacrificed in the process. Sexual addiction has no respect for age, color, race, creed, profession, marital status, sexual orientation, or position of power. Everyone is vulnerable, but it clearly seems to be more frequent in those who have been physically, sexually, and psychologically abused.

A secret well-kept from the general public is the development of the original Alcoholics Anonymous program of recovery, now extended and adopted for a number of other addictions, including sexual ones. As with an alcoholic, the sex addict can be a plumber, lawyer, clergyman, housewife, CEO, or doctor. By contrast, the image most likely to be portrayed in the media is of some crazed maniac who kidnaps a woman and puts her in a box underground.

Steve is married to Gyne and they have children ages twelve, fifteen, and seventeen. He has had a series of women during most of their married life, often more than one at a time. Besides these extramarital affairs, he would frequent strip joints and visit prostitutes when he had a need for sexual release and none of his women were available. His wife threatened to leave him when she found out what had been going on. (This happened when she found a motel key in his pants pocket and demanded an explanation. Later, he reflected that he was so miserable he may have needed to get caught, and this was one way to do it.)

Steve discovered that Sexaholics Anonymous like Alcoholics Anonymous provides a spirituality, not a religion. He and his wife were raised in a mainline denomination but had never practiced their faith. Steve began to attend church regularly with his wife, which he credits to his sponsor in SA and his own desire to make the decision to get into recovery. SA is forcing him to face up to his past and to admit that he had lost control over his whole life, not just part of it. He admitted his powerlessness and turned his life over to a Higher Power. He first had to overcome some false understandings about God from his childhood and culture. He took a complete inventory of his life and admitted his addiction to himself and others. He is now in a process of restoring his marriage to what he had imagined it would be when he first married. It is a slow process for him, but he attends SA meetings faithfully and has begun a prayer life with daily meditation. He has dropped his old activities that were not healthy for his spiritual life. Even though he considers himself sober from his acting out sexually, his SA meetings are a part of his weekly routine.

Steve discovered what a lot of men and women in AA and similar programs discover regularly: they find God in the mess of their lives and come to a healthier lifestyle that replaces the old pattern of bad habits, lies, and deception. Many have found that spirituality is essential for coming out of the darkness into light.

. Unfortunately, addicts frequently have to "reach bottom" before they see their helplessness, damaged lives, and destroyed relationships and can bring themselves to this point of surrender. There needs to be a shift from the apparent object of satisfaction to the real Object of satisfaction. This is not accomplished without considerable pain, but many addicts will testify that it can be accomplished. We can become addicted to almost anything, but the only addiction that is truly safe is the love of God as each individual sees God. Only God is big enough to satisfy all of our cravings.

Chapter 9

Sexuality, Fantasy, and Tradition

To consider the teachings from the Bible and Tradition is part of the proper formation of our consciences. I have placed so much emphasis on the part that fantasy plays in our lives that I wanted to raise it as an issue of morality as well. It may indeed be that the religious Tradition holds us to a more restrictive standard of behavior for holiness than psychology requires for mental health. Some of the more recent biblical studies, however, may have interpretations more aligned with psychology than with Tradition, at least for certain passages.

According to Tradition, we can sin by deliberately entertaining impure thoughts. Biblical statements often used to support this notion are such phrases as "Whoever looks at a woman with lust has already committed adultery with her in his heart," "Blessed are the pure of heart for they shall see God," and "Thou shalt not covet thy neighbor's wife."

Psychology encourages people to be very open about what goes on mentally. Self-awareness and mental health are very closely allied. Psychology discourages repression of ideas and feelings, that is, unconsciously putting them out of awareness without dealing with them. It encourages suppression of ideas and feelings, this is, consciously holding them in awareness long enough to deal with them to whatever extent is possible at a particular time. It may be necessary to set them aside temporarily so as to channel energy in other directions. They can always be brought back later. An aid is to express in words how one is feeling, especially when feelings are intense.

Psychologists usually think of guilt and shame as more appropriate for intentions and behaviors than for thoughts and feelings. However, many feelings of guilt and shame feelings do accompany fantasies. It is not often easy to see exactly where these painful emotions are coming from. Psychology places importance on intention and plan, not on what one is feeling or wishing for. Feelings and wishes need to be accepted, sometimes investigated, understood, and often expanded to other issues. There are big differences psychologically between the wish to kill oneself or someone else, the intention or plan to do so, and actual suicide or murder.

One of psychology's concerns is that a thought or fantasy may be labeled as a sin prematurely and then be resisted as a dynamic issue that is telling us something important about our lives. An example might be a sexual fantasy that is looked on as sinful, causes one to feel guilty, and is then repressed. In this case the fantasy may never be contemplated long enough to reveal that it contains more anger than lust, and that the anger is the more important feeling to deal with, and that doing so can reduce the lust if adequately understood. Neglect of such dynamic issues frequently plays a part in development of a sexual addiction. A very common phenomenon is for one to feel guilt or shame about a fantasy or feeling and then, out of guilt or shame, actually perform some sexual act.

Larry was a twenty-three-year-old male who was married and had one child. He had started having intercourse in high school, which continued in college. Early in college he and some friends would spend time looking at pornographic movies. These were very sexually stimulating and would lead to masturbation when he was alone. The fantasies and memories of these films were hard to get out of his mind because he would feel guilty for even thinking about what he had seen. After a while he began to get these movies for himself and frequently would spend lengthy periods of time watching them and relieving his sexual tensions by masturbating. After he ejaculated he would feel guilty and disgusted with himself for what he had done, and again, he would view the video to relieve himself from the pain and guilt caused by watching it. There could be several episodes of this cycle before he would bring himself to take the video back, resolving not to do it again. He had hoped that getting married would put a stop to the habit, but he soon found that if he was deprived of sex by his wife the pattern would return. He would usually do it while his wife was away. He came to therapy after his wife came home unexpectedly and caught him in the act. She threatened to leave him if he did not get help.

He was finally able to break the cycle by accepting that he could have sexually stimulating fantasies of beautiful, sexy women and not feel that this was wrong. He was even able eventually to see them as real people who were beautiful creatures of God with lives and stories of their own. This detoxified his attitude and his compulsion to regard what was sexy and beautiful as sinful, and it increased his regard for women immensely. Underlying Larry's guilt and shame, obsessive fantasies, masturbation, and pornography were his unresolved feelings over the loss of his mother, who died when he was young. Behind the images of partially clothed women was the one woman who made him feel secure. He was eventually able to recognize that his sense of insecurity, which he felt particularly when he was alone, would diminish as he felt sexually aroused. Mental freedom was necessary to break up his compulsive behavior, but the reflex judgment of sin was the first defense that needed to be challenged.

Biblical studies since the 1940s seem to offer less literal interpretations for the passages quoted above. The first thing that is suggested is that biblical quotes not be taken out of context. For example, the verse regarding lust (Matt. 5:28) and the one about being pure of heart (Matt. 5:8) were both taken from the Sermon on the Mount, the latter from the Beatitudes. Matthew was trying to portray Jesus as the new Moses for the Jewish Christians. He is presenting Jesus as radically different from the Pharisees, who were very much action-centered in their morality. Jesus was sending the message that it is what is happening interiorly that counts. It would be fair to say that Jesus was more person-centered than action-centered in his morality. Being "pure of heart" did not refer to chastity exclusively as it is so often interpreted, but to *right intention,* a singleness of purpose, directed toward God's Lordship. The heart was not seen as the center of emotions for the Hebrew people as it is for modern Christians, but as their conscience, again emphasizing the importance of interiority. The ninth commandment, "Thou shalt not covet thy neighbor's wife," is best viewed in context with the tenth, "Thou shalt not covet thy neighbor's goods." The more accurate meaning for both is, "Thou shalt not covet to possess," which brings in the idea of intention, purpose, or plan to acquire. Psychology is concerned that we befriend our sexuality. Theology looks on sexuality as a gift from God and not something to be feared that will drive us from God. Psychology and theology need to complement one another when it comes to helping us deal with our sexuality. A similar attitude was discussed in terms of sexuality and spirituality. A spirituality must fit our sexuality if we are to develop both.

Two feelings that psychology and the Bible regard similarly are forgiveness and its opposite, resentment or revenge. "Revenge is mine, says the Lord," is often very hard to allow when we feel injured and have a strong desire for revenge, but the wisdom is unquestionable. Forgiveness is particularly hard to achieve when that injury has occurred because of some physical or sexual abuse. To manage this resentment, psychologically speaking, is sometimes very difficult. There must first of all be a clarity about what has happened, an awareness of the reality of the situation, and a recognition of what feelings were associated with it. Because of the natural tendency to repress unpleasantness as a child, accurate memories for traumatic experiences are not always available. Likewise, repressed feelings of betrayal, shame, and often guilt are not easily available. Forgiveness is not even approachable until these other feelings are first dealt with.

Recently a phenomenon called false memory syndrome has developed. As the name implies, a person has a "memory" for something traumatic happening, usually sexual, often perpetrated by an adult, often by a family member, relative, or close friend, that is in fact a fantasy and not a memory of an actual occurrence. It can be quite confusing if it happens to be the memory of an early fantasy. It occurs, not only because of the natural tendency at times to confuse fact and fantasy but because of a therapeutic zeal. Therapists recognizing that remembering is very important for healing might pressure clients to produce memories prematurely and face their traumas before they are ready. This pressure can actually result in fabrication that can be very damaging to the patients and those they accuse, many times their own family members.

Children are particularly vulnerable to suggestion about traumatic events. There have been actual experiments where children have been repeatedly questioned about sexual touching by adults and with each interview new and more vivid details get brought up about what happened in response to some leading questioning.

Once this clarity of memories has been obtained there is usually a need to work on self-respect, shame, the inappropriate feelings of guilt, and anger or revenge toward the perpetrator of the assault. Lawsuits have been brought against parents at times on the basis of these accusations, and some parents have gone to jail. The psychological benefits of such actions may be mixed, but often the individual is left with anger that persists for years, continues to destroy their life, and can be dealt with only by finally forgiving the parent.

Lorraine was a twenty-nine-year-old woman who has been in and out of hospitals several times. She had made several suicide attempts and had been in therapy intermittently for years. She had been sexually abused by her mother, who had given her very frequent enemas as a child. From this trauma Lorraine developed the habit of anal masturbation. During one hospitalization after she had attempted suicide, it became clear to everyone, including the patient, that the only one suffering from the trauma of the past was Lorraine. Her self-images and her mother-images were so fused that when she hated her mother she hated herself, and this usually would lead to some suicidal gesture. As she was able to appreciate that she needed to forgive her mother in order to end her own suffering, a sense of peace began to develop and her mother could be forgiven. This occurs very frequently in the therapies of traumatized patients, but the bottom line is that we do not live happily with chronic anger and vengeful thoughts. We do live peacefully with forgiveness of others and ourselves.

Returning to the Beatitude "Blessed are the pure of heart for they shall see God," it strikes me that the newer interpretation of having the right intention, a singleness of purpose directed toward God's Lordship, is in fact a way of seeing God in our present lives. When we contemplate God as Creator, we are confronted with marvelous and moving truths. Out of the limitless number of creatures that God possibly could have created, we were created, you and I, together with others to share these moments in time. "With age-old love I have loved you" (Jer. 31:3). This acute awareness of God's Presence as Creator of us all provides the foundation for a loving relationship with God and with each other that dignifies our sexuality: "in whom we live and move and have our being" (Acts 17:28). It can be the motive for the other seven Beatitudes if we see ourselves and others as equally special in God's eyes. We will not be inclined to use each other as sexual objects in any sense of that word if we see ourselves as creatures of God to be loved and not abused. I personally think that it adds to our integration. With the internalization that God is central and that we all revolve around God, we stop seeing things in terms of rules and regulations outside of ourselves that we must follow and fear transgressing because of guilt. We value our own giftedness and that of others. This stays with us at all times, directing all of our actions. For Christians there is the added incentive of being able to see others as Christ. "What you did not do for one of these least ones, you did not do for me" (Matt. 25:45).

Chapter 10

Sexuality and Celibacy

I have chosen to discuss sexuality, celibacy, and marriage after sexuality and spirituality because their foundation lies in that discussion. Attempting celibacy without developing a spirituality that is quite profound is doomed to failure. Sexuality in marriage that isn't fueled by the spiritual is likely doomed either to mediocrity or failure.

It is typical for those choosing celibacy to struggle in varying degrees at different times of their lives to keep this public vow. Given that one has had a normal psychosexual development and has achieved the capacity for intimacy and intercourse, celibacy calls for the suppression of direct genital expression. Those who achieve this will testify that at least two major things are necessary after one has made a firm determination to follow this way of life. One must have a life of prayer and meditation, and not just one of ministry. One must also have a variety of ways besides ministry in which to channel sexual and aggressive drives. Celibacy must not be seen as an end in itself but as supplanting sexual energy for the Kingdom of God. This mission provides the focusing powers for all of one's energies and requires that individuals achieve the stage of generativity in their psychosexual development.

Besides the vow of celibacy that religious order priests and religious brothers and sisters make, there are also two other vows that become part of spiritual development, namely, the vows of poverty and obedience. Diocesan priests make a solemn promise of celibacy but are not bound by the other two vows. What strikes me as psychologically significant about these vows and promises is how they all seem to involve a degree of detachment and a movement in the opposite direction from our normal developmental drives. Obviously celibacy requires a detachment from persons with whom genital expression might be possible. Poverty requires a detachment from belongings and properties that are so important to many of us. And finally, obedience requires a detachment from our own willfulness, which is often achieved in a healthy sense after many hard battles. The various healthy attachments that are part of normal character formation and psychosexual development are put to the test. I say healthy, because if these attachments have not been made, the person may be suffering from some kind of a personality or neurotic disorder and will really not be capable of making a meaningful profession of vows. They are really not clear on what they are giving up. When persons take a vow of obedience who have never been able to make up their own mind, there may be a problem later, as there are with adolescents who decide they have to separate psychologically from their parents by making their own personal choices. A similar reaction may occur with personal possessions.

The following is an example of a priest who managed to achieve the celibacy he desired, only to lose it later in life. Father Bill struggled to control his sexual drive the entire time that he was in the seminary. For several years he would occasionally masturbate while in the seminary and would do it more frequently while he was home for summer vacations. He was often attracted to women, and on occasion would date them with some kissing and petting, but he had no sexual intercourse. He managed to control these impulses for a couple of years before ordination and for twenty years after ordination. He felt that he had achieved the degree of celibacy that his vows required of him and was grateful to God for this very special gift.

Then something happened. He was asked to leave a very active parish where he had been an assistant for several years and where his life was filled with a sense of joy and fulfillment as he performed all of the priestly duties and administrative tasks required of him. He was transferred to a rural area where he had two parishes to cover with no assistants for companionship and parishioners who were interested in little more than Sunday Mass. He became a priest who was available for baptisms, funerals, weddings, and not much more. His life was suddenly changed. There were many long and lonely hours with little to do. His former friends were miles away and quite busy with their own lives. He began to experience a sense of emptiness that he carried around most of the day. He lost his appetite, lost weight, and in desperation to get himself to sleep at night he started to masturbate. Before too long he was also using it to relieve the emptiness that filled his days, but the more he tried to address it in this way, the more empty he felt. About this time he also met a very attractive young woman who greatly admired him and was very needy herself. They started to fill the emptiness in each others' lives by engaging in long hours of conversation, affection, and eventually passion and intercourse. Suddenly the hard-won chastity that he thought he had acquired was now surely lost, and besides the other painful feelings he had, guilt now added to his burden. He sought psychiatric help when he felt that the suicidal ideas that he was beginning to have might be acted upon.

He was diagnosed as suffering from a major depression and needed to be hospitalized. He required medication, psychotherapy, and another assignment to complete his rehabilitation. He never wanted to leave the priesthood and eventually was able to see his romantic involvement as symptomatic rather than a serious relationship that he wanted to follow into marriage.

As stated earlier, there are two major drives, sexual and aggressive. It is quite possible for one of these drives to defend against the other. There are certain individuals who might be known to be chaste or celibate, but with further inquiry we can see that they are in fact very mean and uncharitable individuals. Such an individual might even be joked about as someone who needs to "get laid." These individuals have managed to totally repress their sexual drive, but its energy heads down what might be considered the aggressive channel, with a resultant mean-spiritedness that makes them difficult to be around. They are unhappy with themselves and everyone around them.

The same phenomenon can happen in reverse. An individual who is claiming to lead a celibate life is in fact quite sexual. There can be a number of sexual encounters with the need for constant sexual satisfaction. What is remarkable about such individuals is that they cannot get in touch with their anger, often repressed, toward authority figures or members of the opposite sex. We can legitimately ask, "How can a man be making love to so many women and be thought of as hating them?" The answer is that he is not making love to them. He is using them to discharge sexual and aggressive energy and doesn't really care much about them at all. In fact, their being so frequently discarded after sexual relations is a manifestation of this hostility. In such cases the celibacy might even become a kind of shield against real intimacy and is used to rationalize avoidance of real intimate or permanent commitment. (It should be pointed out that this phenomenon is not restricted to men; women can also repress their anger and become hypersexual as well. One common manifestation of it is seen in those who have numerous affairs or engage in prostitution.)

A story I have heard more than once is that of a priest becoming emotionally and sometimes sexually involved with someone he has been seeing in spiritual direction or counseling. It is often a woman, but it may be a man. It invariably happens for either of two reasons. One is the lack of any appreciation of the phenomenon of transference and the other is some degree of psychosexual immaturity.

The particular kind of transference here is to an authority figure who is admired as powerful. It is often a party to what is called a fiduciary relationship, one of trust with a person of some privileged position in the community: a priest, doctor, teacher, lawyer, or boss in a work setting. The person will be regarded as exceptional for his knowledge, understanding, compassion, availability, or personal attractiveness. The individual seeking help is often someone who is very needy and lacking in self-esteem.

Spiritual direction starts off innocently enough on both parts. In fact, the priest is often young and will be imbued with the enthusiasm of youth. He will be very zealous about the welfare of his charge and the welfare of others as well. The person being counseled almost immediately starts to feel better and shows signs of emotional and spiritual progress as soon as things get underway.

Signs of difficulty arise rather slowly and sometimes almost imperceptibly. Sessions get extended a little longer for very legitimate reasons or are held more frequently. Sitting closer happens for various reasons. Sometimes requests are made to meet outside of the usual places or invitations for social activities are offered. A chance pair of tickets to a play or concert appears. An invitation to dinner seems like a reasonable social thing to do.

Even the more dangerous signs of physical contact can be rationalized or ignored. A greeting kiss or hug can be a sign that an emotional bond is growing that becomes more evident as time goes on. Hugs become more prolonged, occur more frequently, or become part of offering some consolation during a session. In fact, things can be happening so imperceptibly that the two people involved sense it all as very natural, loving, and quite legitimate.

This process can be understood in terms of boundaries that are being slightly crossed, but at some point it becomes clear that there is a serious type of boundary violation and emotional involvement becomes obvious.

Father Clarence had been seeing Donna for over two years. Spiritual direction started out at one-month intervals and then was increased to every two weeks and finally to once a week. She had him over for dinner a few times and there had been extensive mutual sharing. He had felt some obligation to repay her for her kindness and had taken her to a couple of concerts and a play. Each was increasingly on the other's mind, but they never confronted their developing intimacy directly.

Ignoring warning signs came to a abrupt halt one night. They became acutely aware of trouble. They were saying goodbye and embracing. Slowly Clarence slipped his arm below Donna's waist, and they both became overtly sexually excited. Neither wanted to speak about what was happening. Amid a range of emotions, something had clearly changed and for many reasons both wanted to pursue it.

Clarence had never had intercourse nor engaged in any petting. He had dated some before the seminary but had never passionately kissed a girl. He had periodically felt deprived of not having had these sexual experiences, which are commonly referred to as experimentation, but he always felt that his celibacy and priesthood were more important. Suddenly, now, under the pressure of passion, his resolve was crumbling and he began to feel like a sexually starved man.

Donna's story was similar. She wasn't very popular and had only a few chances for dating. She did well in school and always prided herself on her academic and professional achievements. She gave little consideration to her psychosexual development. More recently she had even begun to feel her spiritual progress under Father Clarence's direction was a special blessing from God. But suddenly she felt passion as she never had before and wanted to hold nothing back from Clarence.

They managed to separate that eventful night after recognizing that they had touched each other, literally and figuratively, in a new and different way. They each felt the need to think things over, but when they met again in two days there was no turning back. They both were committed to full sexual expression.

The details of this kind of story might vary, but the essentials are always the same and need to be understood. The fiduciary position can frequently stir up strong emotions and sexual desires on both parts. When these are not faced by both parties, they can become very dangerous, and, if acted upon, quite destructive in many aspects. Once they have been faced, they can be consciously dealt with. Of course, the sooner they are recognized the better. Keeping appropriate boundaries will not necessarily keep them from arising altogether, but the boundaries will always keep them from being acted upon. Sometimes it is necessary for these feelings to be overtly discussed between the parties, but the one in a fiduciary position should always discuss them with a trusted friend, colleague, therapist, or spiritual counselor in order to receive support and direction in handling them. If they are not dealt with, they will invariably interfere with the real purpose of the relationship.

It is the basic responsibility of the one who holds the fiduciary position to guide the process. If this cannot be done, the relationship needs to be terminated. I might also add that if these feelings are dealt with properly and boundaries are not violated, it can be a growth experience for both parties. Having trusting relationships that provide a holding environment for whatever emotions arise while perspective and control are established is part of maturation. This is what one hopes happens in families as children mature. Likewise, it becomes destructive when there are boundary violations in families as well. Inappropriate expression of aggressive impulses or sexual impulses by parents causes considerable damage to children.

A rather curious thing often happens once the line of sexual prohibition has been crossed. The power that the priest held is diminished, lost altogether, or even shifted to the person he is involved with. A form of intimacy develops in which the woman or man feels more entitled than before. There is an expectation of more frequent phone calls, visits, and even regular sexual exchanges. These expectations may or may not be conflictual for the counselee, but they invariably are for the priest. The counselee will begin to feel resentment if these invitations for more intimacy are denied. The priest soon feels the guilt of violating his celibacy.

More often than not he does not want this to develop into any type of permanent relationship. He senses the control that is being exerted and feels resentment beginning to well up in him as well as fear about what can now happen because of the turn the relationship has taken. Covert or overt threats might begin to surface.

If both parties can recognize that what happened should not have happened and both can take responsibility for it, a more favorable resolution can be achieved. More often than not, complete separation is required and even desired to overcome the painfully conflicted emotions involved. Less frequently, some kind of a nonsexual friendship can be preserved.

If the counselee, whether woman or man, feels violated (which usually is accompanied with a feeling of rage and of being abandoned) he or she will be inclined to use the power acquired over the priest in some destructive way by informing authorities or seeking some type of lawsuit. The priest will then lose his reputation, position, or both.

When this sad outcome occurs it invariably happens because the priest has rejected, demeaned, or accused his directee. This comes from the priest's own anger and confusion about the whole situation. Shakespeare said, "Hell hath no fury like a woman scorned," and its application here is painfully clear. If the priest treats the woman with dignity and respect and is willing to take more than his share of responsibility, her anger is often lessened, her self-esteem preserved, and her vengeance diminished.

There is a well-known entity in human experience and the analytic literature called the erotic transference. It refers to the tendency to quickly develop erotic feelings toward whomever the transference is directed. It originates from a person of significance from the past, as transference suggests, but its distinguishing characteristic is the easily eroticized feelings meshed with the much less conscious and more difficult aggressive feelings. Such individuals often will not be aware of any negative feeling at all, but are filled and sometimes overwhelmed by positive and often sexual desires. Individuals who become enmeshed in an erotic transference will often find themselves on the receiving end of this anger and aggression when the relationship spoils, as it invariably will. It will fail not only because these kinds of relationships are not sustainable, as in the fiduciary situation, but because within the individual who possesses the erotic transference the repressed hostility is waiting to emerge and will easily be stirred up with provocation. More than one psychotherapist, clergyperson, lawyer, physician, or boss has experienced this most difficult situation. Unconscious hostility can be felt and observed more easily than it can be dealt with.

It is not unusual to have an erotic transference matched by an erotic countertransference. This is where the psychotherapist, clergyperson, or other person in the power position is dealing with a similar unconscious hostility from his or her own past significant figures and is easily inclined to erotic feelings. We can appreciate that if both individuals are carrying baggage from their past, they are very vulnerable to slipping into a relationship that will be not only sexualized, but filled with rage. A priest with this kind of difficulty must receive proper therapy immediately or he will repeat it again with another woman or man sooner or later. If there is no intervention it can become a pattern with much pain and destruction for all parties involved.

Chapter 11

Sexuality and Marriage

My first impressions of marriage, as for most of us, were formed by observing my parent's marriage. It was quite unique in some ways. My parents were childhood sweethearts. They grew up a couple of blocks away from each other in a small Italian Catholic community in Denver. My father was only a few months older than my mother. They went through grade school together and were clearly in love by the time they graduated. My father attended two years of business school before he entered the business world at age sixteen. My mother went to beauty school and became a beautician. Neither ever dated anyone else nor had any desire to do so. They married when they were eighteen and eventually had three children. They were very fortunate to have found their ideal other, as will be explained later on.

My parents' marriage seemed to follow the admonition of St. Paul: Husbands, love your wives; wives be subject to your husbands. My mother was subject to my father, from all that I could gather as I sensed the way things were around the house, with one peculiar exception. Perhaps because my mother was a beautician, she loved my auburn hair and, against my father's wishes, wanted to keep it in a "page boy" style, bangs in the front and long all around. My father tolerated this until I was about three. Then one day he took me to the barber shop and told the barber to give me a regular boy's haircut. When we returned home my mother dissolved into tears. My father simply said that the barber's scissors slipped. But from that time on, I had a regular boy's haircut.

I never realized just how much my father loved my mother until she died at the early age of thirty-six. He was inconsolable. I will never forget the blanket of white roses covering her coffin with a gold inscription, MY DARLING. His obvious grief went on for months until the first

Thanksgiving after her death, when my uncle told him in no uncertain terms that he needed to stop thinking about his wife and start thinking more about his three children. My uncle did make an impression. My father started paying more attention to us, but he did not start thinking less about my mother. Every Sunday for the longest time, we would drive to the cemetery to visit her grave. While she was alive my father would call her every day at noon. Before she died he promised her to continue that practice through the wires of his rosary which he faithfully said every day at noon. He never showed any interest in another woman.

My parents were a product of their time and culture. My father worked. My mother stayed home and took care of the children and kept house. They were both very strict and very loving. They had no problem with physical discipline and certainly did not consider it child abuse. Their view was almost the opposite. If you do not discipline your children when they are little and can step on your feet, they will step on your heart when they are older. I wish that I had the chance to argue with them about the physical discipline part, but I could never argue with them about the love. That was undeniably present and clearly beneficial for all three of us.

Having had something of a Pauline image of marriage in my parents, I was inclined to repeat it with my wife. I recall one very beautiful evening walking with my future bride and discussing our plans together. The sky was clear, there was a soft warm breeze, and romance was in the air. We started talking about what it was going to be like when we were married, mostly about how wonderful it would be not ever having to be separated. Not being too long out of the seminary, I had a lot of Scripture quotes readily at my finger tips. It seemed a good time to show my devotion to her by quoting from the famous saying of St. Paul in Ephesians 5:25: "Husbands are to love their wives as Christ loved the church and delivered himself up for her; and wives are to be subject to their husbands." I was trying to emphasize the "husbands love your wives" part, but she immediately picked up on the "wives be subject to your husbands." This stopped her dead in her tracks, and my fiery little nurse bellowed back, "I am not going to be subject to you!" It was the first time I witnessed some spine in her that I would really come to value very much over the years. But at that moment I was stunned. Hadn't she heard me? I was quoting Scripture. I was quoting St. Paul. I was telling her how much I loved her and what I would do for her. Certainly to be subject to someone who would love you that much could not be a bad thing.

That argument did not get settled that night nor for many years. We needed each other very much, and based on that we got married, figuring that we would work things out. In time I came to understand the instinctive correctness of her response. She knew without being told that there was something unsavory about subjugation. I myself came to appreciate that there was something wrong with it. First of all, if we really love someone we do not desire for that person to be subjugated. We want partnership. We want mutual respect. We do not want fear or intimidation. We do not want to impose but to elicit cooperation. I discovered in many of my patients that subjugation could easily lead into a sadomasochistic relationship, with the wife and husband both locked into defeating patterns.

It took even longer for me before I could differ with St. Paul, but I have come to understand that subjugation and loving can be understood in a different way. Later translations of St. Paul even seem to indicate that, being subject to, could really mean to "listen to." I can heartily agree with that, except that it needs to go both ways. True, wives must listen to their husbands, but just as importantly husbands must listen to their wives. If there was every a repetitive and debilitating pattern that I continually saw in the many couples that I treated, it was that they did not listen to each other. I often felt that if I could get just one thing accomplished in the therapy, that would be it. Listen, really listen to each other, and feed back what you have heard. There is something very confirming when we sense that we are understood, and something very infuriating when we feel that this is not happening. Preparing the counterresponse before taking time to process what has been said and to show an appreciation of whatever emotion is being displayed is an essential first step in communication. There will be plenty of time to get one's own feelings out, and chances are they will be better understood if there has been prior listening and appreciating. Arguments can go on for hours and get nowhere due to this communication flaw.

In a recent moving with Bruce Willis and Michelle Pfeiffer, *The Story of Us*, this communication flaw was demonstrated to perfection.

Criticisms were never taken constructively for whatever truth they might contain, and the occasion for countercriticism of equal or greater intensity was never passed up, so the battle would escalate. Insight into that kind of a destructive pattern does not come easily, and changing it is even harder. But without that change, the marriage is doomed. Someone once described a neurotic marriage as being like two porcupines trying to get close to each other.

I would say that the more we listen to our partners and respond to what is being said, the more the love part of St. Paul's admonition will be evident. I am not suggesting that listening is tantamount to agreement. In fact it often is not. But it is the basis for serious discussion. Exchanging ideas openly and giving each other the time to digest, appreciate, differ respectfully, and move toward some compromise, if necessary, is all part of marital survival.

With a divorce rate of over 50 percent, we have a strong need as a society to look into the causes of this social disaster, primarily because of the effects that it has on our children, and secondarily because of the effects that it has on the parents themselves. Statistics show that second marriages end up more often in divorce than first marriages. For many, it takes the third marriage to achieve a degree of permanence. I recall the attitude of a woman I was seeing who had been through two divorces and was involved with a man she certainly wanted to marry. His ambivalence about commitment, even though they were very active sexually, prompted her to tell him, "I want all of you or none of you." That was for her a hard lesson learned, and probably not a bad bit of advice for those in dating relationships that go on unresolved for years.

I would not suggest that children are better off in a family where the marriage is not amicable, although there are those who would argue for this, asserting that children need stability more than amicability. Some children are clearly better off, safer, and happier when they are out of an environment of intense parental conflicts, especially when there is physical or sexual abuse. What is necessary is for couples to delay marriage until a sufficient degree of psychosexual maturity has been achieved, or to get into therapy as early as possible when this may not have been the case. It is clearly possible to save some marriages; others it is not. I can recall one of my senior analytic teachers saying in a strong German accent, "There are some marriages that not even a thorough psychoanalysis can save. It may even be necessary in some cases to bring about a divorce."

The issue that needs to be addressed here is the influence that psycho-sexual development has on marital happiness and stability. If either the man or the woman has significant emotional or sexual immaturity, the marriage is in trouble. Emotional immaturity can be manifested by such things as a volatile temper, excessive dependency on a spouse, irrational jealousy, a lack of trust that is unfounded, the need to have one's own way all the time, and sexual or substance abuse and addictions. Very basically, it is not being able to see what one's spouse needs for his or her emotional and physical well-being or, having seen it, not being able to provide it. A marriage requires that individuals be interdependent and that each be able and willing to shoulder the responsibility for the family in whatever way can be mutually agreed upon.

Today, the work issue is as important for the woman as for the man, not only because most families require two incomes to survive in to-day's society, but also because women have found that developing their personal talents is just as important for them as it is for men. I am refer-ring to survival not in terms of luxury, but basic things such as housing, clothing, education, medical, and dental treatment and eventual retire-ment needs for the couple. The working mother needs the father to assume household and child care duties, which many husbands are not only willing but quite able to do. If both parties are not equally carrying such responsibilities, resentment or anger develop, which can go in many different directions. These kind of responsibilities cannot be carried out by immature people.

Sexual immaturity is often manifested by such things as very little sexual desire, particularly in newlyweds, varying degrees of impotence or premature ejaculations on the part of the man, or painful intercourse or frigidity on the part of the woman. If these and other similar issues are not attended to early in the relationship, whether they are discovered before marriage (if the couple has been living together) or after if there has been little or no sexual experimentation, the marriage is in trouble. These difficulties need to be distinguished from a kind of developing compatibility that most couples go through as they discover their pref-erences and limits with respect to sexual behaviors. The difference is that this kind of adjustment takes place between two people who have sufficient sexual development, and therefore the necessary flexibility, to enter into sexual intimacy with someone they love. I am concerned about those who for whatever reasons do not have this potential for developing sexual compatibility. It may require some consultation to help in making the distinction.

If there is ongoing or unresolved conflict or dissatisfaction over any sexual issue, it often becomes a major factor in the deterioration of a relationship. The issue can be that some sexual desires are chronically unsatisfied. (It is assumed that these desires are considered to be within the normal range of acceptable activities. If they are not, then there is a clear need for consultation.) One frequent complaint is that one partner desires intercourse much more frequently than the other. This is a common cause for infidelity. Another is that the quality of the sexual foreplay is lacking in some ways. (Here is where establishing genital predominance and a range of pregenital or foreplay activities as discussed in the chapter on masturbation is important.) For example, if one or the other partner has a need for passionate kissing or oral sex, and the other is unwilling to participate, sexual frustration and tension can arise. If one partner is capable of self-satisfaction but lacks the interest or ability to help satisfy the other partner, tensions will arise. Parenthetically it might be mentioned that dealing with these difficulties is often not easy because of a reluctance of many couples to talk about them, either with each other or with a therapist. There is a need to explore and establish which sexual activities are acceptable and which are not, so that sufficient sexual satisfaction can be obtained and the necessary agreeable compromises can be made.

Again, we are able to see how the issue of anger can arise from sexual dissatisfactions as it did from not adequately sharing responsibilities for the family. Often the anger is what surfaces, while the sexual dissatisfaction goes unaddressed.

How is anger dealt with? In many different ways. It can be overtly expressed with outbursts, chronic fault finding over insignificant matters, staying away from home, and emotional distancing. It can be covertly expressed by starting an affair, squandering money without the knowledge of the spouse, or spending more and more time at work. Anger will eventually destroy the love feelings that brought the couple together and led to marriage in the first place. It needs to be dealt with early on, before it destroys more than can be repaired and continues to mask the real underlying issues.

Transferences play a significant and often unrecognized part in marriages. Transferences were considered in detail in the chapter on sexuality and spirituality. It can be shown with detailed exploration that the problems in most marriages are related to unresolved transferences in one or both partners. We refer to a henpecked husband or a submissive wife. Of course, there are counterparts — the controlling wife and the dominating husband. It is usually not very difficult to determine where the attitude came from by looking into the backgrounds of such individuals. They have identified with parental figures who played those same roles in their own families. What is often of interest is that such marriages can work as long as people stay within their assigned roles. The wife or husband must remain subservient if the other is to be dominating. When they begin to grow and start to refuse to be treated like a child, then chaos erupts. This is when people head for therapy or divorce courts. This kind of marriage will inevitably break up if only one party wishes to change and grow. If both are willing to give up their transferences from the past and see each other as they really are, then there is hope. If such a marriage does not change, chances are that the children will identify with their parents and enter neurotic relationships or marriages themselves later on.

A word needs to be said about transference as it relates to children who have experienced a divorce in their families. They often will be suspicious that they will be abandoned by someone and erect protections against this happening. It might mean a fear of even getting involved, or it might mean a premature early involvement designed to undo the sense of aloneness and abandonment that resulted from the divorce. The tragedy here is that often the partner will be selected more on the basis of internal need without adequate attention being paid to the person's potential to really become a satisfying adult partner. The discrepancy is discovered only after the incompatibilities and conflicts arise, and children of a divorce who vowed they would never behave like their parents find themselves in a divorce court, worrying about what they might be inflicting on their own children.

The most important thing to keep in mind about transferences reactions is that they are not engraved in stone, although at times they might seem to be. They are behavior patterns laid down in earlier life by repetition, often in a manner that is unconscious to the person developing them. If an individual can come to appreciate that there has been some unconscious identification with a parental figure in an unhealthy way, the potential for change exists. Once the behavior is isolated and recognized as undesirable, a more suitable behavior can be put in its place. I must also add that this may result in more rather than less conflict for a while. For example. If a woman has allowed herself to be terrorized by her husband because she learned that a woman is to be subject to her husband, even in an unhealthy way, there will be trouble when she begins to stand up to him. In extreme cases there can even be physical violence, but usually this is not the case. She needs to get a message across that she matters, her opinions matter, she needs to be heard, and she is prepared to seek with him a better way of communicating. In a healthy scenario, this can even be welcomed on some level by a husband who has become disgusted with his own bullying behavior. He may likewise need help to see that he matters, his opinions matter, and he needs to be heard. He just does not need to use the tactics that he probably learned in some transferential reaction from his own youth.

Moral issues can become problematic in the process of trying to establish sexual harmony. A young couple starting out needs to be able to make love without shame in the presence of God who created us, and not in the presence of a judge who is interested in whether they perform sexual acts correctly. In the chapter on contraception, I discussed some of the problematic aspects of requiring that each and every sexual act be open to the possibility of conception. As stated earlier this requirement is based on the principle in Thomistic natural law theory that the male seed must be deposited in the vagina when the couple engages in sexual intercourse. The teaching further states that any sexual behaviors between the couple are permissible provided that the male seed is deposited in the vagina. This of course refers to passionate kissing, touching various parts of the body, masturbation, and oral or anal sexual acts.

Encouraging a broad range of sexual behaviors will certainly enhance lovemaking and allow the couple freedom to establish the sexual patterns that can carry them for a lifetime. Requiring that the seed be deposited in the vagina each and every time may not. Here is why: When the couple is making love they need to be focused on what is mutually pleasurable and stimulating and not when ejaculation is going to occur, except as it might be related to that end. (A priest friend of mine described a professor of moral theology in Rome as coining the term "spermadola-try" — an idolatry of sperm as characteristic of the church's teaching on sex.) We have another version of an action-centered morality versus the person-centered. Couples are required to focus their attention in a way that does not foster mutuality. The main focus is on the man's readiness for ejaculation, and not on their mutually agreed upon time for insertion and later ejaculation. Why should this be a problem? It may be a problem for the woman if she is not sufficiently stimulated and her husband insists that he is ready and fearful of ejaculating. It may become a problem for the man if he sees performing in such a way that it can cause anxiety and consequent premature ejaculation or even impotence. Lovemaking must be completely free and mutual. When or how an ejaculation happens should not be a moral concern. If the anxiety and guilt can be eliminated a man is quite capable of restimulation and completing another act of intercourse. What is critical is a sense of lovemaking in which the interpersonal issues are attended to. If this is done in a loving and caring manner, there will be more than enough intravaginal ejaculations.

There are times when a couple may choose to make love but not want to have full intercourse. If either partner has an infection, they may wish to make love but not necessarily have intercourse. On these occasions some form of masturbation would be appropriate. (Again, this would be prohibited by the requirement of intravaginal ejaculation.) There may be times when a man is reluctant to have intercourse but willing to give his wife an orgasm, which even for the woman is thought to be permitted only as a part of the act of intercourse. The whole issue of oral sex can become inhibited if the couple is not free to opt for it, whether as an end in itself or as preliminary to the act of intercourse.

Another significant factor in the success or failure of marriage is the issue of attachment, which was considered in the chapter on sexuality and spirituality. Overattachment can operate in marriages, and many times it takes the form of trying to force the other to be what we want them to be. One of the interesting things in most romances is that a person falls in love with two people. One is the person in reality and the other is the image of their ideal love which seems to have been found. Early on these can be fused into one with infatuation, but may separate out as the relationship progresses. We may tend to seek the magic we feel in the presence of our ideal and then begin to feel disappointed as the real person emerges, not measuring up to this ideal. This can lead to many struggles as each person tries to show his or her real identity in the presence of the other who is doing the idealization. If the real person is valued more than the ideal, the marriage will thrive as the ideal is given up as not as valuable as the real. Obviously, there must be enough of the ideal in the real person to keep the basic attachment intact. What is necessary is for each to see the other as a person with all that implies: a life story, psychosexual development to whatever level it has been attained, goals and aspirations, human needs and frailties, a spirituality to be respected, and a partner with whom they wish to share life. When that is achieved there is no question that true love begins because the other's good is truly sought.

Marriages are often troubled by an idealism with regard to a sexual partner better than the one someone is married to. This is often a sign of immaturity when such fantasies are taken seriously. We certainly have an ample supply of such "beautiful people" in our culture, and the temptation is always there to be looking for something more unless we are wise to the pitfalls. A recent statement on the Internet said, "The next time you see a beautiful woman you would like to seduce, remember that there is a guy somewhere who is tired of having sex with her." A few days later another version appeared: "The next time you see a beautiful woman that you would like to seduce, remember that there is a guy somewhere who is tired of taking her 'stuff.'" I am sure that the ladies could formulate the same notion about a good-looking guy. These statements confront the unrealistic expectations we place on sexual enjoyment. We expect that the sexual excitement that exists early in relationships will go on forever and that relationships are not supposed to have boredom or "stuff" in them. I think that these unrealistically high expectations about sexual pleasures, and the low tolerances for the discomforts of living with another human being with inadequacies and imperfections, say something about the failure of marriages. If these attitudes are not challenged and something more meaningful put in their place, I don't believe that the divorce rate has a chance of dropping. Much of this really is a matter of psychological education and not allowing the media to have free reign to promote whatever it might be trying to promote without some countervoice.

Here is where spirituality and maturity come in. Having the ability to see and follow through with one's spouse's physical and emotional needs is the essence of love coming from the loving Spirit of one's beliefs. The Spirit is quite capable of competing with the most exotic of sexual pleasures that can be keeping us from a wholesome and committed relationship, if that is required, and will bring a very sustaining peace of soul that sex can never produce. The Spirit helps us tolerate human frailties in many ways, most importantly I think through the example of tolerance the Spirit shows to all of us.

We are all familiar with the Christian teaching: What God has joined together, let no man put asunder. My first thought is, What kind of a man would want to put asunder what God has joined together? It needs to be determined what God has really joined. I personally do not believe that God joins together two immature people who are pledging themselves forever without having really developed psychosexually and learned what commitment really means.

For most people, and I would include myself in this, real commitment does not take place when they make marriage vows. It occurs sometime in the course of the relationship when they realize that this is the person they are really committed to and will remain with for the rest of their life. Often it occurs after there have been trials or temptations. It occurs after one has appreciated that there are some discrepancies between the ideal and the real person, the ideal is recognized exactly for what it is, a mental image, and the significant other is recognized for exactly who he or she is, the person I really love.

As I suggested earlier, for my own parents (and I am sure it is true for others) the maturation occurred very early. The ideal and the real for them happened to be one and the same. It can be legitimately objected that maturity at such an early age is a contradiction. I would have to agree, but it must be pointed out that maturity in one aspect of our personality doesn't necessarily mean maturity in all aspects. In fact, a person can be very mature and capable in some areas and lacking in maturity in others. Still, for them and many others, falling in love takes place just once, and it is known to be genuine early on. The significant issue is that it is known to be genuine and never seriously doubted. When this kind of internal sense is achieved and agreed upon by two people, that, in my opinion, is when God joins them together.

Chapter 12

Sexuality and
the Roman Catholic Priesthood

As a psychiatrist, I have always been interested in the social factors that influence behavior. They can be just as powerful as the biological, psychological, and spiritual forces that lead us to behave in the ways that we do. Evolution and revolution have us always changing. This change may not be evident for centuries, but at times like our own, changes can be staggering. Primitive humans wrote and painted on their caves. Today we communicate in cyberspace. Primitive people survived with minimal clothing and were hardly able to protect themselves from the elements. Today we live in temperature-controlled environments. Revolutions seem to stem more from inner needs that are often of such importance that we will die for them. We are seeing a type of revolution in the women's movement in our time. For centuries, women were content to be in the positions men placed them in and felt that it was right because of their gender. They disregarded the emotions that might have rebelled against it. This is clearly not the case today. There is an ever-developing clarity that sex has nothing to do with female potential, and that the prevailing attitude was imposed by men so that men could be in control. To put it simply, women are on the move and no longer willing to be controlled.

Prejudice against women is as old as history. Women were declared unclean because they menstruated. Women have been treated as the property of men for longer than many of us would like to admit. When celibacy was established by the church and some of the wives objected to losing their husbands, they were sold into slavery or sent to a convent. What an unholy start! Women had to be kept in their so-called place for years because of a fear that they would deprive men of their powers by sexual entrapment. (This may well relate to a primitive but not uncommon male fantasy of the so-called *vagina dentate,* a vagina with teeth.) Women fulfilling the role of seductress have often been seen as more sexually alluring and therefore more dangerous.

Women were considered for many centuries, because of the lack of scientific knowledge, as being only incubators for the male seed, which was thought to contain a small human being. It wasn't until the 1850s that the advancement in medicine could prove otherwise. Psychoanalysis has also perpetuated ideas of the incompleteness and inferiority of women because they do not have a penis or because they seem to have certain masochistic traits in their character that predispose them to suffer abuse. It took some very astute women analysts to challenge these psychological beliefs, just as it has taken some very astute women theologians to challenge the theological beliefs about women and priesthood. There is no turning back the clock.

If there was ever a time in history when women seem to be breaking through the so-called glass ceiling that keeps them from positions that heretofore have been occupied only by men, it has been during the last half of the twentieth century. Women have entered the competitive world of international team sports, become United States senators and CEOs of large corporations, and participated in the exploration of space. When I went to medical school, out of a class of one hundred, there were six women. Now there is frequently a fifty-fifty split of males and females in medical schools. The number of women theologians is growing by leaps and bounds. More women are getting college and higher education degrees. Previously, only the males of a family were thought to be worthy of an education. Women have entered all of the various professions and skilled labor positions.

Perhaps the most influential positions assumed by women are in politics. They are bringing a feminine perspective to an area where it is badly needed. Their ability to communicate more freely and their tendency to use their aggressive drives less than most men are bound to bear fruit as time goes on. Their nurturing instincts will be effective in public policy. A woman who has borne a child will be much less inclined to go to war than a man. Women priests could bring a similar perspective to the priesthood as they did to the military. The military prides itself on being a peacekeeping force as much as a fighting force. Women, I believe, are better at peacekeeping than men. They are much less concerned about themselves and their prestige than men are, much less isolative and defensive about their feelings than men, and their nurturing qualities carry far-reaching beneficial effects. The church at times has considered itself as a military force: the Church Militant, the Church Suffering, the Church Triumphant. The Crusades were certainly a military operation and not one of our proudest moments by Gospel standards either. The better qualities of women's personalities can only enhance our church and our priesthood.

It is hard to imagine any place where women are not given the opportunity to achieve besides the priesthood of the Catholic Church. It must be pointed out that educated and accomplished women in the Catholic Church are no novelty. Many religious sisters have excelled in hospitals, colleges, and universities. The women of the Episcopal Church finally won their right to priesthood, and there are in fact now women bishops. I recently spoke with a woman deacon in the Episcopal Church. She said that she does not at this time wish to become a priest. She feels that her life is full enough with the good works she is able to do as a deacon, but the option of becoming a priest is at least open for her.

Vatican II's Constitution on the Church states that the priest acts "in the person of Christ" (39). This teaching goes back to Pius XII's encyclical on the liturgy, *Mediator Dei* (1947), and is also found in the reforming Council of Trent, session 22. According to the official church teaching, the issue is not a mere biological distinction between male and female. The crux of the pope's argument following Vatican II is that the male priest images Christ "as head of the church."

The rational arguments that the pope proposes for not ordaining women are not convincing to many men and women. Despite the denial that it is a male-female issue, it is clearly the maleness of the priest that is being noted "in the person of Christ" and not Christ's person. If the person of Christ were the focus, we would consider such issues as His compassion, his devotion to the will of his Father, his zeal for souls, and his love for humankind even to death on the cross. His maleness pales by comparison to those qualities, which are ideals that are not restricted by gender. Unfortunately, there have been many male representatives of Christ as "head of the church" who have been sadly lacking in the character of Christ.

The fact that something has not existed in the church is no reason why it cannot be introduced (if it is not an essential doctrine of belief). Since the Spirit is guiding the church through the ages, such an introduction could easily be conceivable given the cultural and value changes that continually occur.

In conversations that I have had with educated women from other countries, I have been told the seeds for change are there and have been sown in some places, but there is still a long way to go. One bright sister from Central America in discussing women's issues said, "We are poor because we have very few material things, and we are poor because we are women." That speaks volumes of how women are regarded in some cultures. It will take some time before the old beliefs die and women are judged more for their gifts than their genitals, but the momentum is unquestionable.

In this country, Susan B. Anthony, Elizabeth Stanton, and their fellow workers strove for seventy-five years before they could get laws passed across this country that gave women the right to vote, the right to own property, and parental rights. They were disregarded, demeaned, and considered as only evidencing their inferior mentality by even asking for such rights. Women were very supportive of the abolition of slavery, no doubt because they felt something in common with the slaves, but slavery was abolished before women were given their rights.

The twenty-first century has been declared by the American bishops as a time for special renewed emphasis on social justice. It will be only a matter of time until the inconsistency that exists between social justice teaching, as advocated outside of the church, is seriously considered as a matter that needs to be dealt with inside the church as it pertains to the ordination of women deacons and priests. The shortage of priests will certainly fuel this fire. However, it seems more likely that the celibacy laws for men will be changed before women will be ordained. Already many former Protestant and Anglican pastors who are married are being ordained to the Roman Catholic priesthood.

It would probably be easier for everyone if Christ had said that he did not want women ordained as priests and deacons, but he did not. His commandment was that we love one another. In fact, it is inconceivable

to me that Christ would not have wanted women priests at some time
in history. Christ was love and compassion personified. He forgave the
woman at the well, he cured the woman from her hemorrhage, and he
allowed a sinful woman to wash his feet with her tears and wipe them
with her hair. Would this same Christ not want women to share in his
salvation wish for the world by bringing him to the world as Mary his
mother had done in the beginning?

It seems much more likely to me that Christ did not ordain women
among the apostles because of the culture of the time. Women then
were not allowed to attend synagogue services. Women were not regarded very highly in terms of their rights, talents, or abilities. They
were to be protected. He was choosing men for a dangerous mission.
They were to go forth to preach the gospel to all nations. It was as if
Christ were selecting a nonviolent army, and women were certainly not
part of military operations in those days. Women on such a controver-
sial mission would have been in grave danger. But to conclude that his
intention was more than temporary is fallacious.

The magisterium argues that the call to the priesthood is a gift from
God, not a privileged political or human right. I see nothing in that
argument that says the gift cannot be given to women if the hierarchy
were to so choose. Celibacy is likewise a gift from God, and many
women through the years have been so graced.

The more we study the similarities and differences that truly exist
between men and women based upon nature, the more the prejudices
will fall away. I would not be surprised if it were considered an "intrinsic evil" to deny ordination to women in the future. We concede that
God wanted all humans to be saved — that baptism is available for all.
Salvation was to come through other humans who loved God enough
to bring the Good News to the world. Does it really make sense that
half of the human race that Christ came to save would be denied an
expression of that love by being excluded from his ministry or ordained
priesthood?

Priesthood is an empowerment beyond belief: the power to call God
down upon the face of the earth, the power to forgive sin, the power
to heal mind and body. It is inconceivable to me that men would not
want to hoard that power, particularly if women even unconsciously were
viewed as a threat to its integrity. What a movement could be created

for the one, holy, catholic, and *apostolic* church if women began to share fully in evangelization. The whole world needs women, and women need men to speak with them and for them. Women need to feel good about themselves, which many of them have not been able to do, and men need to take some responsibility for women's lack of self-esteem. What a blow to the worldwide prejudice that still exists against women if the Catholic Church were to declare that She loved her daughters enough to offer them the gift of priesthood.

Women have barely begun to exert pressure themselves for the priesthood. There are still many women who believe that the priesthood is for men and that they have no right to it. There are others who claim they would not accept priesthood with the hierarchical structure being what it is today. They see the church as needing to be much more Christ-centered than power-centered. Women will push more and more for priesthood — and probably in the not-too-distant future. A couple of things need to be kept in mind. First, women are the predominate churchgoers. This can be easily observed by attending any given church function. It is more predominant in some cultures than others. Second, women are the mothers of priests. Many a priest has entered the seminary because of his mother's influence. Once women begin to feel that there is an injustice in the priesthood and that they have daughters as well as sons who should be considered worthy enough to become priests, the tide will shift. The influence on sons to be priests, sometimes subtle, sometimes strong, is disappearing and with it a certain number of vocations have already been lost. If women so choose, they can have a very strong financial effect on the church, both in terms of being givers themselves and in the influences they will bring on men to withhold support. Hopefully, changes will come before these kinds of tactics need to be employed.

The current worldview of the Vatican is to maintain a male priesthood because many Third World countries have seminaries which are quite full, and it is easy enough to project that such seminarians can become missionaries to other countries, as has happened with so many Dutch, Irish, Polish, and Spanish priests in the recent past. The problem is that many of these young men are drawn to the priesthood because of the status and financial security which it affords. This has already been demonstrated to be a mistake, both in terms of those who leave before ordination, and those who leave after ordination. These countries need their own priests who understand and value their culture, just as we need priests who understand and value ours. At the same time, these are countries where women themselves have not yet felt liberation in its fullest expression.

An issue that is getting some attention, and will certainly get more as time goes on, is the increasing number of priests who are homosexual. The present rate has been estimated to be between 25 and 50 percent, with the higher percentages being among the younger priests and seminarians. I personally have known many homosexual priests and can say that they are often intelligent, talented, gifted, and spiritual men. Their ability to function well in the priesthood is undeniable, and often their appreciation for suffering is very keen because of what their orientation has required of them.

To understand the reasons for the number of homosexual priests would require a thorough study that to my knowledge has not been done. We can speculate that it is either because more heterosexuals are leaving the priesthood or because fewer are entering the seminaries. It may be that there is a growing awareness of the presence of homosexuals, in the clergy. It may be that the priesthood is becoming a more comfortable place for homosexuals considering that they have been shunned by so many groups in the past.

How much this trend will continue is obviously open to question. One thing that I hope will come from it as their numbers increase is that it will pressure the hierarchy to challenge the notion of labeling homosexuals as having an "objective disorder." That label really helps no one. It can only demean those who have a homosexual orientation and prejudice those who are inclined to be homophobic.

One particularly negative aspect of the homophobic prejudice is that it may deter heterosexuals from entering the priesthood, which as everyone knows is approaching a state of crisis. Perhaps this increasing percentage of homosexuals in the priesthood may prove to be one of the elements that will help to abolish the requirement of celibacy for ordination to the priesthood. If seminaries could accept male and female, homosexual and heterosexual, there would be an abundance of laborers for the harvest and many of these inconsequential issues would disappear.

Chapter 13

Sexuality, Aging, and Death

Wilma lived in an apartment by herself. She was an elegant, talented, and tragic older woman who came to me for brief episodes of therapy and medication for depression over several years. She had been a musician and played cocktail piano for several years in New York until she came to Washington, D.C., in search of a more stable career. She found her way into the executive secretary level of the government and had several high-level bosses. Her advancement was in no small measure due to her dedication and long hours of work. She finally retired, but her personal isolation was catching up with her.

She never married or had children and was an example of someone who was "married" to her work. She had a series of lovers who provided her with some companionship and sexual satisfaction, but these relationships always ended for reasons that were never clear. I had the impression it was largely due to Wilma's fear of real intimacy. Her system of work, lovers, and professional advancement sustained her for many years, but when she retired it was not from a job, but from life. She had nothing to love and nothing that she could believe in. Her health began to fail, her mind became disturbed, bordering on the psychotic, and she could no longer care for herself. The last time I saw her was prior to her entering a nursing home. The move was being engineered by the manager of her apartment house who was aware of her increasing disabilities.

When I was in psychiatric residency in the early 1960s we were taught that it just wasn't worthwhile doing intensive therapy on people after the age of fifty. It was felt that they were too inflexible to change very much, and we should probably consider doing intensive therapy with people

167

who had a longer life expectancy. I do not recall what life expectancy was back then, but I do recall that it was a rarity to find someone who had lived over the age of one hundred. Today there are hundreds of centenarians and life expectancy is increasing all the time.

What is significant about our changing attitudes is that we no longer consider age a deterrent from doing anything if one has the motivation and physical health to engage in it. This includes our sexual lives as well as our professional, personal, and social lives. This broader view of our potential is extremely important to prevent the tragedy exemplified by Wilma's life. From early on, we need to see ourselves as having multiple potentialities and cultivate all aspects of our personalities and talents. Probably the most important of these, and the one so missing in Wilma's life, is a capacity for intimacy. If we do not have this connectedness to others, and I would say most importantly to the God of our faith, we will suffer and deteriorate rapidly. I have become convinced, as I have seen my own life unfold, and watched what happens to others, that the true saving grace is having a meaning or purpose for existence. Without it, there is no reason to get out of bed in the morning at any age. There is no joy or enthusiasm for living. There is no caring for oneself or anyone else.

Obviously retirement is the most dangerous time. The satisfactions and responsibilities of a position that keep many of us going are no longer there. The income stream from steady employment is cut off, and retirement incomes are often not adequate for anything beyond the bare necessities.

What does sexuality look like in old age? Fortunately, or unfortunately, it looks very much the way it did when we were younger. I read an article written by a widow who described her attempts to cope with her loneliness and sexual frustrations after the death of her husband. Clearly she had a very satisfying marriage, but after the mourning for her husband had passed, she felt very needy. She was so attuned to her cravings for affection that she was alarmed at the amount of sexual responsiveness she felt even by embracing her female companions. She found periodic relief from sexual tensions through masturbation, but the deeper longings for a real relationship were constantly present. She wrote the article to call attention to the false concept, believed by many older women, that once their husbands die it is expected that they become asexual.

We need more knowledge in this area. One could easily suggest that remarriage is the answer for those individuals who feel so inclined, but there are many complicating issues.

Clifford was a widower I had started to see for depression after the death of his wife. He had been a deacon for a few years and was giving some thought to entering the priesthood now that his wife had died. It seemed like a way to fill his emptiness, but it also didn't seem quite right. He had recently met Anne, who was a widow, and they felt a very strong attraction toward each other. As his depression lifted, Clifford thought less about entering the priesthood and more about marrying Anne. But there was a problem. Because both of them were very devout Catholics they wanted to be married in the Catholic Church. The problem seemed insurmountable. Clifford became a deacon before there was any expectation that his wife would have an early death. Deacons have to make a promise of celibacy in the event of their wife's death. He knowingly made the promise, but what he could not have known then was what it would be like to be a widower and to fall in love with someone who, like himself, had developed the capacities to be more loving and sexual through a previous marriage. When he applied for a dispensation from his promise of celibacy, it was denied. After several attempts, they decided to take personal responsibility before God for their love and commitment and had a civil ceremony. They both also started to attend the Episcopal church.

The two purposes for marriage are unitive and procreative, as stated earlier. With older people the procreative end is no longer an issue. The question then might arise as to whether they are required to act sexually in their marriage as younger couples are. Is a man who is impotent and no longer capable of intercourse allowed to pleasure his wife and bring her to climax? Is a woman who finds intercourse very painful for a variety of reasons allowed to do the same for her husband? Using the "intrinsic evil" model for determining the morality of sexual acts, these actions would not be permissible.

There are people who are able to commit to each other and who desire an ongoing intimate and sexual relationship, but who do not wish to marry again for a variety of reasons. One might be the loss of pension benefits that would occur with a remarriage after the death of a spouse. Another might be the unwillingness to give up independent living conditions that have been acquired over a lifetime of work. Some find serious difficulty with their children's feelings. Is there some way that these people can find some sanction in a relationship that will satisfy the needs of older age that isn't geared toward providing the environment for raising children and the stability that requires?

Television shows periodically depict older women who have been taken advantage of by con artists who rob them of their money and valuable possessions. The cons are able to prey on their vulnerabilities and get them to make financial concessions after they are convinced that they are loved. I think such vulnerability is a testimony to the importance of sexuality in the lives of older people as well as the potential consequences of living in isolation, where that kind of vulnerability can be exploited.

Chapter 14

Sexuality and Pedophilia

As humans we have a strong desire to know, but in certain situations we have a remarkably strong desire not to know. It took airliners being flown into the World Trade Center before we could acknowledge our vulnerability to hostile forces penetrating our nation. It has taken an ever-widening scandal of child sexual abuse for us to acknowledge that criminal acts have been covered up by the church hierarchy out of a fear of the stain of scandal.

In 1985 a detailed study of the national problem of pedophilia was written by F. Ray Mouton, a Louisiana lawyer who defended the first priest legally accused of pedophilia, together with colleagues, Rev. Thomas P. Doyle, a Vatican canon lawyer, and Rev. Michael Peterson, a psychiatrist. The following statements were reported in the *Washington Post* (August 4, 2002):

> They drew on reports and medical articles, and filled the report with advice on screening and treating priests, and how to handle allegations of abuse. They suggested forming a rapid-response team that would travel to troubled dioceses and advise officials on strategy.
>
> The men implored the church to make a new covenant with the faithful. The alternative, they warned, was a blizzard of lawsuits that could cost the church $1 billion.

The accuracy of these predictions is uncanny, and it is indeed tragic that this report was suppressed. Now is the time to acknowledge that sexual education and sexual formation within the church have some broken parts. We can't help but wonder what can be going on when those who have received the best of what Catholic sexual education and spiritual formation have to offer end up sexually abusing those who have been entrusted to their care.

The problem did not occur overnight and will probably take months and even years to eradicate — if this is even possible. Reduction and control may be all that we can ultimately hope for.

Xavier was a teenage seminarian who was struggling with masturbation. He frequently confessed his mortal sin to his spiritual director, who instructed him as follows to control this perverted behavior. When he was troubled by this temptation he was to come to his director's room. There he was to lower his trousers, bring himself to full erection, and the two of them would pray before the crucifix that he would be released from this temptation. When his erection subsided he was allowed to return to his room with the instruction to returned if the temptation re-occurred. This went on for some time until Xavier told his director that he could now control himself. This of course was really not the case.

There were many horrifying aspects to this story. Xavier left the minor seminary with considerable doubts and scruples about his sexuality. He started having relations with women and this assured him of his masculinity. After a failed marriage he spent many years in therapy working out his own psychosexual development before he arrived at some peace and a place where he was able to have a successful marriage. Besides the damage that was done to Xavier, what needs to be considered is the tragic denial and repression of sexuality in his spiritual director, who from all appearances to Xavier had come to believe that this was truly a way of helping a young boy prepare himself for chastity. What of course went on with the director after Xavier left his room is not known.

For the sake of clarity, let me note that child sexual abuse refers to a number of sexual acts that occur between an adult and a child which are appropriate only for adults, such as intimate kissing, intimate touches and oral, genital, and anal intercourse. Although children are capable of varying degrees of sexual stimulation, they are not capable of handling the confusion and stimulation that is initiated by an adult, particularly an adult who is trusted and in some cases even loved. Psychologically and physically they are ill-equipped for such activities.

Let me begin by acknowledging the many good priests who have not been afflicted by pedophilia or any other kind of sexual disorder who are now suffering with a kind of shame by association. They are looked upon with suspicion, and many have become afraid of the most innocent physical contact with children. They are just as important in our evaluations as are those who have such difficulties. They will help to delineate the redeeming as well as the damaging factors which are causal in these tragic cases. One of the major problems in this whole area is that there has been repression on the part of the hierarchy, not only of cases of pedophilia, but of studies which could shed more light on the subject of sexuality. When I thought about this topic, I went to a very comprehensive book entitled *Catholics on the Internet* by Brother John Raymond. Astonishingly there were no direct references to pedophilia. When I first tried to publish this book I was told by one publisher that his house could not publish it because it would be taken from the shelves by the bishops.

Let me also clarify that I do not think that pedophilia is a problem due to celibacy, although celibacy may play a part, as I will discuss later. Pedophilia has been a problem that cuts across many lines including clergy and laity, married and single, young and old, educated and noneducated, professional and nonprofessional. Perpetrators can be parents, relatives, family friends and neighbors, caretakers, teachers, doctors, married and single individuals, heterosexuals or homosexuals. The range of individuals involved would indicate that we are dealing with factors operative not only within the Catholic seminary system of education, but factors at large in the culture. The point that I would emphasize is that the Catholic seminary system as it has been operated in the past has not offered sufficient psychological screening for individuals with pedophilic propensities, nor has it offered spiritual formation, which would assure that with ordination candidates had achieved a degree of maturity and psychological development sufficient to allow them to be safe caretakers of parishioners, particularly children. The expectation would be that the incidence of pedophilia among the clergy would be much less than that of the general population.

I do not think there is any doubt that the entire Catholic community, hierarchy and lay alike, have become attuned to the need for changes in seminarian development and are presently responsive to this problem. What concerns me is that, after the acute phase of pointing fingers at the guilty and making reparation for the past, there will not be undertaken the hard work of identifying the sources of these problems and what must be challenged in the system of beliefs and practices to ensure that not only cosmetic changes are made.

I can no longer look at children who have been abused without wondering what profound psychological damage has occurred that will affect them in future years. How will the memories logged in their conscious or even unconscious mind affect their ability to form intimate relationships and color the pleasures of their sexual life. There will be unexplained fears, inappropriate guilt, disturbing fantasies, or all-to-vivid memories of confused sexual feelings that began long before they were ready for them.

We do not thoroughly understand the causes of pedophilia, but there are some things which are clear. One of the most disturbing consequences of sexual abuse is when the abused becomes an abuser. One of Freud's most helpful discoveries was of the mental mechanism called identification with the aggressor. This simply means that whenever we are on the receiving end of an aggressive action, our unconscious will record it, and then we have a template for the same or similar aggressive actions ourselves. The golden rule of "do unto others as you would have them do unto you" is more likely to become do unto others what was done to you. The words "violate" and "violence" have more in common than similar derivation. They both deal with transgression of another human being, albeit in different degrees. The tragedy of abuse is that it is often not regarded as violating by perpetrators. In fact it is often seen as caring and loving. The problem is that the so-called "loved" child is not capable of that kind of overextension of emotional and physical capacities, which results in their not being loved at all, but victimized.

Not everyone who becomes a child abuser has been victimized. The range of factors that can cause retardation in psychosexual development discussed earlier will apply here as well. Of note is the absence of appropriate sexual objects during one's adolescence. If there are no female adolescents in the environment for proper heterosexual development, individuals will be at risk. This fortunately has been recognized by the church and the so-called minor seminary has been eliminated in this country. Minor seminaries were willing to take boys in to study for the priesthood right after grade school. Here they were often not allowed any relationships with girls, they might have been overstimulated by other males, and, most distressing of all, they might enter into an abusive relationship with seminary instructors, as the case of Xavier demonstrates.

When discussing homosexuality, I said that the more proper term would be "homosexualities" because the notion covered such a wide variety of behaviors. The same could be said of pedophilia. We really have pedophilias. Let me just describe some of the variables. The victims can be toddlers or teenagers. When the victims are post-pubescent the disorder is often referred to as ephebophilia. Frequency is an important issue. Some individuals will engage in a few acts as part of developmental experimentation and then draw themselves away from the behavior. Others will be involved in years of consistent and frequent activity with a number of individuals, and there will be all gradations of involvement between those two extremes. Some individuals feel guilt and shame for their behavior, which may or may not lead to effective rehabilitation. Others feel little of either, and this usually leads to recidivism. (One thing is always clear for all psychiatric disorders. Treatment is ineffective for anyone who does not want to change.) Some individuals are stimulated only by children, others only by adolescents, some by children, adolescents, and adults. Some are stimulated by those individuals of the same sex, others by individuals of the opposite sex, and some by either sex. Given these complexities we must be clear that one size does not fit all. Each case requires careful, thorough, and prolonged evaluation if we are to see that a correct diagnosis is made, an adequate treatment plan is formulated if appropriate, and a just sentence is imposed for the range of crimes that can occur with these disorders. A much more detailed discussion of these issues can be found in an excellent article by Father Steven Rossetti in *America* Magazine.[34]

The difference between pedophilia and ephebophilia is a useful one. It distinguishes between child abuse which occurs with a prepubescent child, pedophilia in the strict sense, and child abuse which occurs with an adolescent, ephebophilia. We can see that there is a big psychological difference developmentally between a man having sex with a fourteen-year-old girl who looks eighteen and a man having sex with an eight-year-old girl who is naïve and trusting. The former is clearly a person who is more developed in his love object choices than the latter, but still lacking in the full maturity required to enter into a sexual relationship with an adult female.

What are some of the other possible factors in the lives of priests who have been found guilty of child sexual abuse? The arrested sexual development might have been perpetuated by religious prohibitions against careful examination of their sexual thoughts and feelings during the years of seminary training because they were labeled as sinful. They might have been further handicapped in any early resolution of their conflicts by the lack of trained people who could have helped them or, worse yet, by mentors who would in fact engage in sexual activity with them. They often would show a kind of subservience to authority figures which would make them seem like good candidates for obedience, a virtue valued in both religious orders and the secular priesthood.

As the crises of pedophilia and the shortage of priests mounts, the attitude of the church, which is so against an open discussion about sexuality issues or literature that challenges church teaching on sexuality, must be overcome. Clearly, efforts at change have been made by many individuals, but the fear of hierarchical reprisal has hampered an open discussion that is absolutely necessary for healing and prevention.

In recent years a lot more attention has been given to sexuality and psychosexual development because of the problem of child abuse. This problem has gone on for centuries, but it seems now to be emerging more clearly and in larger numbers and is being addressed in different ways. There is no dispute between psychology and theology regarding the evil of this behavior. Both hold it is seriously wrong, and if the concept of intrinsic evil, so widely used in traditional sexual morality, has any application in today's thinking, it should be with regard to child abuse. There are never any circumstances where it can be justified.

Child abuse is being more clearly regarded not just as a psychological problem which needs treatment but as a criminal act which needs to be addressed by the justice system. Priests will no longer be allowed to have treatment for this problem and given a new assignment without involvement of the justice system. Victims will be more inclined to come forth without the fear of being blamed or shamed and will be able to receive the necessary treatment. The bishops are considering a policy of one strike and you are out. There is certainly a lot to recommend it. However, there are some problems.

There are priests who committed this offense many years ago and have led very priestly lives since that time. To have a blanket policy that such men must leave the priesthood may be too harsh. A recent suicide of such a priest may give everyone cause to pause and see if the one strike application without a certain amount of judgment and justice should apply. Another problem is that putting a priest out with no job, a tarnished reputation, and most significantly no supervision might not be the best way to help society. Might there be some argument for those whose offense might not merit jail time to remain in the priesthood performing some useful function, and most of all receiving supervision and therapy for the sake of society, if not for the individual himself? We do have a record of many men being treated successfully for this problem, primarily of ephebophilia, which could suggest trying some measures of rehabilitation in selected cases.

Pedophilia is a behavior that evokes anger toward the perpetrator and empathy toward the innocent child. There is often a feeling that the perpetrator needs to be punished. This punishment does happen in many ways after a person is caught, or after passion subsides and a glimmer of the wrongfulness of the behavior begins to dawn along with the acute psychological torture that comes from a broken promise or vow. (Granted that there are those who show no remorse, are habitual offenders, have a strong denial of wrongdoing, and lack any potential for rehabilitation.)

There is another issue that merits our attention. Studies show that most perpetrators are themselves victims, so if we were to turn back the clock and focus in on them at a younger age we could see how they were victimized. If allowed, that same feeling of empathy could be directed toward them, and the anger and hostility directed toward their perpetrators. I point this out to show that there is a vicious cycle of generations that needs to be interrupted and that only punishing the guilty will not stop the problem. The solution lies in prevention.

The issue of celibacy and pedophilia is an important one. Celibacy does not cause pedophilia any more than it causes any other sexual difficulty (such as homosexuality or pornographic addiction) where one can argue that there is not an adequate natural release for sexual impulses. The problem lies in the way we deal with our sexual instincts. If they are seriously repressed without being examined and controlled consciously and adequately over a significant period of time while one is preparing for a celibate commitment or any sexual commitment, there is serious danger for eruption later in life while one is under stress. When thoughts and feelings are repressed out of fear, they basically are out of control and a person is at their mercy. When they have been faced and appropriately dealt with, a person is in a safer position to commit to celibacy. Celibacy is always difficult for a normal person. It becomes an impossibility for one whose psychosexual issues have never been explored.

What specifically needs to happen for one to be sure that he will not be in danger of becoming a pedophile? Basically we need to recognize that pedophiles are seeking immature persons as love objects and that attraction is present in their fantasy life. What is essential is that that attraction be recognized in their fantasy life *before* it is ever acted out. (Nothing can be dealt with that is not first of all brought into consciousness.) Then it needs to be discussed with a professional who can help them deal with the inhibitions to acquiring a more appropriate person as a love object, whether that be a person of the same or the opposite sex. If someone is contemplating celibacy, this understanding is especially important, first of all, for their development, second, to determine whether it is motivational in seeking celibacy, and, third, for clarity about any potential risk if the fantasy has any potential for progression into behavior.

It seems to me that a front-page article in the *Washington Post* (June 1, 2002) entitled "Why Is It Tough to Answer in the Priest Abuse Cases" sheds some light on this subject:

> He decided to become a priest at 14, a time when he was horrified by stirrings of homosexuality that were anathema in his "very macho" family. His motives for joining the priesthood are typical of many of the four hundred Catholic clergymen that psychologist Curtis Bryant, a Jesuit priest affiliated with the Los Angeles Archdiocese, has treated. "I think the priesthood has traditionally been a refuge for people who didn't feel sexually adequate and who considered themselves damaged goods in some way and had histories they wanted to hide," said Bryant, director of clinical in-patient services of the St. Luke Institute from 1989 to 1995.

Homosexuality and pedophilia are sometimes confused. A homosexual person can be fully and comfortably developed. Pedophiles are never fully developed and one hopes they will not be comfortable with their sexual impulses. Being comfortable with this immaturity is what leads to eventual acting out of the fantasies and impulses. The discomfort with the pedophilic orientation is the only salvation against acting out and at least puts pedophiles in the frame of mind where they might seek help. Again, this second step is a problem, because it is not easy to talk about such a thing with anybody, particularly not with someone who is assessing you as a potential candidate for celibacy and the priesthood.

Doing a psychological assessment is not an easy task. We like to make diagnoses because they give us a sense of control and understanding. However, a diagnosis done prematurely or incompletely can be dangerous. With diagnoses what is really important is getting into the multiple manifestations and causes of the disorder. Only with this comprehensive approach can we make an adequate assessment of how the person needs to be treated and what dispositions are appropriate. It applies to all assessments, but most particularly homosexuality and pedophilia in this context.

For example, adolescents who have homosexual tendencies should be given space and support to grow out of homosexuality or grow into it as the case may be. If the genes are there they ultimately might not be able to avoid the recognition that they have a homosexual orientation. Others, if given space, might see that it is something only temporarily appealing for different reasons. Still other may come to recognize that they are bisexual and then need to decide how they are going to make their commitments. Time is essential in making the differential and ultimately helping to seek the appropriate mature love object. Those with pedophilic tendencies will never be able legitimately to have the relationship they desire. The goal must then be to help them move on to a more mature love object. If this indeed is not possible, the goal must be to help establish the controls necessary for containment whether that be psychological with appropriate suppressions and sublimation of energies, environmental by never allowing the person to be alone with a child or adolescent, or both.

One of the places where I think ephebophilia is a legitimate concern is in the seminaries. A person with a tendency to homosexuality might very well come out with a young male. This could occur in the seminary years or later on. Here I do not mean to imply anything negative about homosexuals in the seminaries. But this is a matter which needs to be attended to in an open way and help given so that legitimate vocations can be preserved and those who are not suited for celibacy helped to seek a lifestyle which is appropriate for their orientation and personality.

When it comes to the treatment of pedophilias several things can be said. Most important of all is that it is not like an appendectomy where an organ can be excised and there is a real cure. With pedophilia as with most sexual perversions there is always a chance of a relapse into the undesirable behavior because the memory of what was pleasurable will always be there, with varying degrees of intensity, vividness, and attractiveness. The cure rests in the defenses that can be built up over time to establish firm controls so that there will be less and less of a chance for the impulses and fantasies to be acted out.

Because there is such a range of variables in the pedophilic conditions themselves there is an equally wide range in the treatment outcomes, which will vary depending upon several factors. One is the length of time the behavior has been established. The less entrenched the greater the chance of success and the more entrenched the less the chance of success. The attitude of the pedophile toward the condition is a key issue. When a person sees little or nothing wrong with what he is doing the prognosis is very poor. Feeling guilt and shame and the desire for change are very helpful attitudes to have for more successful treatment. It must be added that this desire for a behavioral change must be sincere and not just superficial, appearing repentant to avoid punishment. Unfortunately, genuine regret is not something which comes easily in many cases, and part of the treatment is to break down defenses so a person can have genuine remorse for the damage done.

The intensity of the treatment is very important. More intensive programs, usually in-patient, lasting for several months with lengthy follow-ups are preferable to individual out-patient treatment. The advantage of the intensive program is that it can combine many modalities of treatment. Patients can receive individual and group therapy. There can be behavior modification programs with individuals learning to pair attractive sexual images with less attractive ones to diminish sexual desires. There can be intensive intrapsychic work where the exploring of sexual fantasies can be undertaken and the inhibitions to moving on to more appropriate adult love objects can be explored. Medications can be given, often estrogen hormones, which tend to diminish the sexual drive itself. There can be Sexaholics Anonymous (SA) groups to help with the addictive aspects of the behavior and to establish a peer support system to assist in the moments of possible relapse. It must be emphasized that none of these modalities alone is therapeutic but undertaken together in a well motivated individual the outcome can be quite promising. This can be said more of ephebophilia than pedophilia.

Unfortunately there are further types of abuse going on in the church today that need to be examined. They may be related directly or indirectly to child abuse issues. Abuse can be physical, as in child physical or sexual abuse, or it may be anything that disturbs the psychological, social, or spiritual well-being of an individual or a community. One form of abuse that has Catholics up in arms is that of money and power in the way the pedophilia cases have been handled by the hierarchy. Millions of dollars were paid to lawyers and victims provided the victims remained silent about their abuse. I say millions because the exact amount has not been revealed, but estimates range from three hundred million to one billion dollars. This lack of disclosure and accountability for the exact amount and sources of these funds is part of the problem we face. It will be hard for the hierarchy to reestablish credibility without addressing this issue.

Occasionally we have heard of a diocese that was on the verge of bankruptcy or church properties needing to be sold to cover mounting expenses in settling claims. Many clergymen who knew about these funds and victims who were receiving them were willing to remain silent about the cases for the scandal to be contained or for the money received. A zero tolerance for priests and a one hundred percent tolerance for bishops seems questionable.

A preferable scenario would have been immediate disclosure with profuse and profound apologies and immediate treatment for the victims. Intense treatment for the perpetrator and involvement of the legal system would also have been crucial. The silence without apology and admission of wrongdoing might not have been therapeutic for victims even if financially rewarding. Mental health is always preferable to financial gain as those victims and perpetrators who have committed suicide demonstrate.

To me what seems unconscionable is that this occurs while the church is preaching that preferential treatment should be given to the poor. Every pastor or layperson could point to some need in their community, from physical repair of buildings to a multitude of charities that desperately need more funds. Yet the money was being used to quietly settle cases without any revelation to the faithful. It was greatly feared that the scandalous pedophilic behaviors would be found out. That fear has not only come true, but now there is the additional scandal of how the cases were handled. All of this went on for many years until some of the cases became so outlandish that they could no longer be hidden from public scrutiny. A priest found guilty of abusing well over a hundred children over several years who was repeatedly moved to new assignments precipitated the need for full disclosure of the existing abuse cases in the Catholic system and the demand for apologies and accountability.

Retrospectively it is easy to see that some of this money was badly needed for research on the causes for pedophilia in the clergy and for the training of rectors, seminary educators, and spiritual directors in dealing with it. But research and secrecy tend to move in opposite directions. There is no question that church officials now are trying to rectify these wrongs, at least in terms of overt pedophilia. The big question is how far the hierarchy will be willing to go to deal not only with the acute problem, but to make structural changes. It will be absolutely tragic if nothing happens except an intensification of the spiritual ideals of the priesthood and business goes on as usual. That would indeed be the most comfortable for the hierarchy but the most likely to prove that nothing has been learned as the cases start reappearing.

ANOTHER FORM OF ABUSE occurs with those seeking a Catholic sexual education. There is a painful discrepancy between what is officially taught by the church, what is allowed to be taught by Catholic educators, and what is practiced by most of the faithful. Those who do the teaching, from the teachers of children in grade school to the professors in colleges, will often have to put a barrier between their own personal beliefs and what they are required to teach. What is not being looked at is the effect that this is having on students and teachers alike. Children are not stupid. They can sense when something isn't quite right in the way material is being presented. Evasive remarks do not go unnoticed.

More aggressive adolescents and college students will raise the issues to conscious discussion where, a saving grace will ultimately be found in the principle that the formation of one's personal conscience is a Catholic teaching also. But before that principle is reached, many teachers who disagree with official church teaching on sexual ethics will convey the message, "Don't press me too much on this particular issue because I do not want to get into trouble, nor do I want to get anybody else in trouble." I have had several Catholic educators verbalize that process to me. What kind of a message do our youth take away with that sort of interaction? Is it not condoning a type of hypocrisy for fear of authority? The youth may take away the healthy notion that they need to form their own conscience, but will they take away a respect for our Catholic system? Will they feel that they are part of a system that really hangs together in clarity and freedom, and will they be willing to fight for it and bring others to it? Or will they become more like their teachers and decide: "Many things are really not safe to talk about, so if I have any problem in the sexual area, I had better keep it to myself."

Part of the remedy here does not even have to be a change in the church's teaching. It could simply be to respectfully and completely teach what the church teaches, but to have the freedom to honestly express where one's own reflections might differ. In terms of development that would be better than the evasive actions which are taken now, leaving children to their own speculations.

There seems to be an underlying assumption that if the differences were expressed the students would not listen to the church's teaching. That may be true, given the number of people who do not follow the church's teachings on sexuality. But believing that just hearing the church's teaching will be enough for belief is indeed false in many cases.

MOVING ON TO ANOTHER ASPECT of this problem of child abuse, the psychological professions need to take some responsibility for declaring people fit for returning to ministry when they in fact were not. This error can be made when a professional sees periods of remission in behavior and hears certain insights about behavior that suggest hopeful change, with a determination not to let anything happen again. Clearances have occurred because of the failure to appreciate the tenacity of perverse behavior and the overwhelming power of passion, particularly for individuals whose sexual practices may be associated with frustrations in their daily lives. The human mind is capable of changing in a heartbeat when a sufficient amount of frustration, hormonal increase, and pleasure-enticing fantasies move into place. What is seen in the professional office is very different from what may be seen in the line of passion.

Fortunately those who work in this area are becoming more aware of the intransigence of sexual disorders, which may require years of follow-up to ensure that significant change has taken place. For some there may be complete remission; others may achieve a certain degree of control over fantasies and impulses without acting them out. For others there may be periodic relapses, and for an unfortunate few, no ideational or behavioral modification whatsoever may be possible. These are the cases from which society really needs to be protected.

We can't help but wonder what effect this child abuse scandal will have on a beleaguered priesthood. The most immediate effect will be a further reduction in ranks, which has been occurring since Vatican II and according to some observers has already reached a crisis point. A "no tolerance" policy would result in an acute loss. It remains to be seen how extensive this expulsion process will become as different dioceses follow suit and what course of action religious communities will following with those accused of abuse in their ranks.

It is a fact that some men join the priesthood because of the need to place rigorous restraints on their own sexuality and look to the priesthood to help them with that struggle. One of the dynamics that can lead to pedophilia is seen when the restraints break in a person who is not adequately prepared to deal with sexual instincts. It would be beneficial for such an individual and for society if he were to turn away from the priesthood because it did not offer such a harbor. But again it would mean fewer priests.

When missed sexual development is discovered later in life, it often brings resentment and the wish to make up for lost time. If one is free to do so, developmental issues may be resumed. If one has made a commitment either to celibacy or marriage the problem becomes more complicated.

I hope all of this will lead to the lifting of the celibacy requirement for ordination to the priesthood and the admission of women to the priesthood. It is really time that we stopped acting like celibacy and masculinity are preferred to the Holy Eucharist. There is reason to believe that if celibacy were optional it could regain its merited value for those who had the ability and the courage to live it.

Seminarians would be much freer to discuss their sexual life without the fear that they could not be admitted to priesthood if they acknowledged they needed a sexual partner in their life. It is also possible that with the freedom to discuss options and see a real choice for the priesthood with or without celibacy, some might choose celibacy. It is further possible that those early pedophile tendencies could be assisted in their psychological growth. That growth may require that they find a sexual partner, but they may also become dedicated married priests.

One further troubling thing about celibacy is that often those promising, through no fault of their own, have not had enough psychological development to make a commitment to last a lifetime. I have heard many times the story of sexual awakening in the thirties and forties. If such men were free to marry, many of them would, without going through the anguish of breaking their vows. Others would be able to stay committed to celibacy more readily, despite some periods of confusion, without a lot of interfering baggage. And most important of all, they might be helped from succumbing out of desperation for sexual release to a variety of sexual relationships that bring neither sexual satisfaction that is more than temporary nor a relationship that is truly loving.

It needs to be acknowledged that there has been for the last several years an increased dialogue between the church and psychology regarding the need for seminary candidates to be screened for signs of sexual maturity, the presence of any perverse sexual behavior patterns, and the potential to lead a celibate life. I do not know of anyone who is involved in this type of training and education who feels that it has been as intensive and widespread as desirable. The cases of sexual abuse that have been openly discussed occurred more than ten years ago. This does not prove that there are none more recent that have yet to be disclosed. This might indicate that indeed progress is being made, but we will not know for sure for some time. What has to be kept in mind is that many of those who did practice abusive behavior went on claiming to practice celibacy for many years before the behavior patterns were discovered.

It has taken abused adults to bring this problem to light. That implies that we have been dealing with cases which occurred at some time in the past. A little reflection will show us the difficulties of learning about more recent cases. When abusive sexual activity occurs with a child, the perpetrator usually tells the child to keep what has happened a secret. Whether from fear, love, duty, or confusion the child may very well remain silent, often for long periods of time if not permanently. When the child begins to give the secret away through behavior changes, psychological symptoms, or direct revelations, adults are then in the position to do something. As incredible as this may seem now, some children have not been believed because it was assumed that they were not telling the truth or because their parents simply could not face the reality. Granted that a child now is much more likely to be believed, it is very understandable that a parent (and, I would say, all those dealing with the situation) would not want the child exposed in any way.

Here is where it becomes a real problem to get adequate information about what is going on at the present time. We know that there are presently at least five facilities capable of offering treatment to those suffering from presumed pedophilic disorders. We know that those who are being treated have a right to their privacy and integrity if they have not been convicted of a crime. And no one wants to have a victim, particularly a child, further victimized by exposure to public scrutiny and humiliation. This obviously means that the important information that is needed for understanding is not readily available, to say the least.

Yet in spite of these difficulties, we need to have adequate information about the realities of these tragedies if there is ever to be research, understanding, education, healing, and most important of all, prevention. Ways have to be found in which those responsible for the welfare of children can offer adequate assurance to the parents that this issue is being dealt with. We need to have a Catholic system of education which will allow our young people to develop in a manner that will give them the psychosexual maturity they need to make a healthy and holy life choice for its expression.

Epilogue

Jesus spoke of persons placing their heart where their treasure is. He spoke of a person selling what he had in order to buy the field where he knew there was a hidden treasure. And the Gospel tells of the apostles leaving all that they have in order to follow him. We need a focus in our lives for mental and spiritual health. There is an axiom that goes, "If you do not know where you are going, then any road will do." The biggest problem is deciding what the treasure is. Treasures can be multiple: money, power, fame, sex, relationships, position, being loved, pleasing others, obtaining applause, educating, running a business, raising a family, making a living, seeking God, physical health, beauty, gambling, boozing, or some combination of the above. We try to prioritize and bring into harmony what may often be competing goals. We can do no better than to look toward the greatest commandment, love of God, self, and others as ourselves, as the guiding principle (Matt. 22:37–40).

The love of self and others implies, first of all, an awareness of all four dimensions of our being: physical, psychological, social, and spiritual. The expressions "get in touch with yourself" or "become aware" point to ways to grow and become healthy and holy. When we are afraid of our bodies or our minds we are indeed impaired. When we are afraid of or distance ourselves from others, we are going against our nature as social beings. And when shun God, we go against our spiritual nature. The Vietnamese Buddhist author Thich Nhat Hanh encourages us to look deeply into everything about us. Jesus tells us to look deeply into everything within us. We do these things through the processes of meditation and self-reflection.

In the chapter on the stages of psychosexual development I used this statement at the end of each stage of development: *God unconditionally loves us and simply wants us to love ourselves and each other.* It is a notion that requires volumes, but I would like to give it two paragraphs. To love ourselves requires that we start with who we are, creatures of an all-loving God who not only created us from nothing but continually sustains our existence. We need to recognize that, by nature, we do not owe our existence to ourselves and that we long to live forever as part of that nature. Dwelling on the awesome fact of our dependent relationship on a loving God will inspire us to love God in return. This is also by nature. A child will spontaneously love its parents in response to being loved. Our tendency to love God is an example of how "grace builds on nature," which is an accepted theological principle. We will respond to this knowledge with profound feelings of gratitude and worship. We will want to live as we were made by God to live. A loving child will want to please a loving parent. We will begin to long to fulfill our destiny and will cling to our Creator as our Beginning and End. That is how we love ourselves.

To love each other is to seek to act as God acts to all: with compassion and caring. We will see the immense value in each human being. Prejudices such as race, ethnicity, creed, gender, sexual orientation, culture, accomplishments, and status begin to pale by comparison. We are brothers and sisters of a Loving God. This directs us to act accordingly. And it might be added that those who are the most needy are really the most entitled. In our time I see this as particularly applicable to the poor and to the underdeveloped and debt-burdened countries that have much need for the advantaged to help raise them to their God-given dignity. I also see it as particularly applicable to women, who for the first time in history are being appreciated as equal to men and are entitled to all of the respect, rights, privileges, and love God wills for all human beings.

I have attempted to describe how the gift of our sexuality develops gradually in us through the long process of psychosexual development. This development is complex and, if not carefully shepherded, can result in many difficulties. I have attempted to describe how our scientific and theological knowledge has developed over many centuries, giving us reason to reevaluate our sexual ethical system in light of newer and clearer understandings. Moral theologians are placing more emphasis on the human person in relationships when determining the morality of individual acts. Psychologists study the human person in relationships when determining what is mentally healthy and maturing. Given this same object for study, the dialogue between psychologists and theologians can only deepen our understanding and appreciation of this marvelous un-folding gift from God that we call sexuality. As the dialogue continues we will become increasingly clear about what is truly human, healthy, and holy in our lives.

I can think of no better way to end than with a quote from Richard Gula's *The Good Life* and the beautiful song "O God You Search Me," based on Psalm 139, performed by Bernadette Farrell:

> Jesus tells us that to be human is to discover yourself and to dis-cover God, more by surprise than by intention. It means that to be human is to live with others and to learn how to love and to be loved, how to be one's own person and still be of service to others. Jesus shows us that really to be human and to live morally is to take responsibility for living. It is not to hitch one's soul to another's star or to do what others say simply because they have authority over us. Rather, truly moral living is to say what you believe to be true, to do what you believe to be right, and then to live out the consequences.[35]

O GOD, YOU SEARCH ME

O God, you search me and you know me
All my thoughts lie open to your gaze
When I walk or lie down you are before me
Ever the maker and keeper of my days.

You know my resting and my rising
You discern my purpose from afar
And with love everlasting you besiege me
In every moment of life or death, you are.
Before a word is on my tongue, Lord,
You have known its meaning through and through
You are with me beyond my understanding
God of my present, my past, and future too.

Although your Spirit is upon me
Still I search for shelter from your light
There is nowhere on earth I can escape you
Even the darkness is radiant in your sight

For You created me and shaped me
Gave me life within my mother's womb
For the wonder of who I am I praise you
Safe in your hands, all creation is made anew.[36]

Notes

1. *Catechism of the Catholic Church* (Washington, D.C.: United States Catholic Conference, 1997), no. 907, p. 239.

2. Dogmatic Constitution on the Church, Vatican II, *Lumen Gentium,* no. 12, p. 164.

3. U.S. Catholic Conference, *Human Sexuality: A Catholic Perspective for Education and Lifelong Learning* (Washington, D.C.: United Stated Catholic Conference, 1990).

4. Joan Timmerman, *Sexuality and Spiritual Growth* (New York: Crossroad, 1993), 9.

5. Richard M. Gula, *Reason Informed by Faith: Foundation of Catholic Morality* (New York: Paulist Press, 1989), 220.

6. Ibid., 223.

7. Ibid., 224.

8. Ibid., 225.

9. Ibid., 235.

10. Lisa Cahill, *Women and Sexuality* (Mahwah, N.J.: Paulist Press, 1992), 45.

11. Sigmund Freud, *Three Essays on the Theory of Sexuality,* 1909 standard edition of *Complete Psychological Works of Sigmund Freud* (London: Hogarth Press, 1909), 7:125; Erik Erikson, *Childhood and Society* (New York: W. W. Norton, 1963).

12. Rene Spitz, "Anaclitic Depression," *Psychoanalytic Study of the Child* 2 (1946): 31.

13. Pontifical Council for the Family, "The Truth and Meaning of Human Sexuality," *Origins* (February 1, 1996): no. 69. p. 541, Catholic News Service, USCC, Washington, D.C.

14. Sandra Schneiders, *New Wine-Skins* (Mahwah, N.J.: Paulist Press, 1986), 219.

15. Judith Viorst, *Necessary Losses* (New York: Simon and Schuster, 1986).

16. *Catechism,* no. 1776, p. 438.

17. Ibid., no. 1782, p. 439.

18. Ibid., no. 1783, p. 440.

19. Ibid., no. 2351, p. 564.

20. John Money, *Love Maps* (New York: Irvington Publishers, 1993).

21. John Hollis, *The Eden Project: In Search of the Magical Other* (Toronto: Inner City Books, 1998).

22. Richard Sipe, *Celibacy: A Way of Loving, Living, and Serving* (Liguori, Mo.: Triumph Books, 1996), 184.

23. Ibid., 103.

24. *Catechism,* no. 2352, p. 564.

25. Ibid., 565.

26. Cited by Gerald Coleman, *Human Sexuality: An All-Embracing Gift* (New York: Alba House, 1992), 315.

27. Cited by Vincent Genovesi, *In Pursuit of Love: Catholic Morality and Human Sexuality* (Collegeville, Minn.: Liturgical Press, 1996), 321.

28. Ibid.

29. John Francis and Irvin Marcus, *Masturbation from Infancy to Senescence* (New York: International University Press, 1975).

30. Coleman, *Human Sexuality,* 206.

31. Thomas Fox, *Sexuality and Catholicism* (New York: George Braziller, 2000), 297.

32. Jon D. Fuller and James F. Keenan, *America* (September 23, 2000).

33. Theresa Cavenaugh, "Living in the Presence," *Shalem News* (Fall 1999), Institute for Spiritual Formation, 5430 Grosvenor Lane, Bethesda, MD 20814.

34. Steve Rossetti, *America* (April 2002).

35. Richard M. Gula, *The Good Life (Where Morality and Spirituality Converge)* (Mahwah, N.J.: Paulist Press, 1999), 86.

36. Bernadette Farrell, *Christ Be Our Light* (Portland: Oregon Catholic Press Publications, 1994).